EATING WITH WINE

by the same author

GOURMET COOKING FOR EVERYONE

EATING WITH WINE

Guirne Van Zuylen

FABER AND FABER
3 Queen Square
London

First published in 1972
by Faber and Faber Limited
3 Queen Square London WC1
Printed in Great Britain by
Latimer Trend & Co Ltd Plymouth

ISBN 0 571 09958 0

In Memory of
My Father

Contents

Contents

Maps

❦

Acknowledgements

The completion of this book would not have been possible without the help of the many members of the wine trade, who have given me so much encouragement and advice.

I would especially like to acknowledge the enormous debt I owe to Monsieur Philippe Marion, director of Messrs. Chanson, Père et Fils in Beaune, who so generously gave of his time, experience and hospitality, and who made many valuable suggestions on the arrangement, not only of the wine sections, but also on the composition of the menus.

My grateful thanks to the following members of Messrs. Deinhard & Co.: Mr. Peter Hasslacher and Mr. B. E. Fruer, M.B.E., for their patience in checking the list of shippers, Mr. T. D. Clark for giving me the benefit of his knowledge of port, and Mr. Ian Jamieson, M.W., who reassured me as to the accuracy of my statements on *Appellation Controlée*.

The late Mr. W. C. King and Mr. Bernard Bright of Messrs. Williams and Humbert verified my notes on the Solera system.

The more intricate details of German wine production were unravelled for me by Herr Manfred Völpel, who also meticulously looked over the subdivision on German sparkling wines.

Mr. D. Lovell, M.W., of International Distillers and Victuallers, almost at an hour's notice, showed me a number of representative North African wines, enabling me to describe them at first-hand, as it were.

As I am the world's most incompetent typist, Mrs. Edna Lewis once more took over this very important task, and deciphered my illegible handwriting with her usual skill and forbearance.

Preface

Wine is one of the oldest industries in the world. Since the days of the Old Testament every country has produced some form of wine, and though, over the centuries, progress has inevitably been made in the methods of cultivation and production, the fundamental principles of wine-making have remained unchanged for the past five thousand years.

Here I must make it quite clear that there is only one drink which merits the name of WINE. It is that which is made from grapes. This does not, of course, apply to distilled wines. There are, as we know, the enthusiastic fermenters of fruits and vegetables, and the other enthusiasts, who, like ancient alchemists, carefully nurture their blendings of dehydrated musts (the name given to unfermented grape-juice). But none of these has anything to do with the mysterious processes through which the fresh ripe grapes pass before they are transformed into the elixir which we call wine.

Briefly, wine is grape-juice, the sugar in which ferments and is transformed into alcohol. In general, the people who make it and a great number of the people who sell it are carrying on a tradition whose foundations were laid almost since the world began. It is as much an art as a craft.

The different varieties of grapes, allied to the varying types of soil, and the varying heat of the sun's rays, combine to give us an almost unlimited choice of styles and qualities.

The vineyards of the Moselle valley, the most northerly in the world, many of them composed largely of slate, produce deliciously crisp and elegant wines, whose freshness is matched

by no others. The flat gravelly areas of poor land on the banks
of the river Garonne (which flows through Bordeaux to the
Bay of Biscay), are the nursery of some of the noblest wines in
France. Between these two geographical extremes lies an
infinite variety of wines, from the deep golden intense sweetness and strength of a Tokay to the earthy dryness of a German
'Steinwein', from the lightness of a Chianti to the depth of the
great Burgundies, there is a wine for every taste.

Taste . . . what is it?

'I know nothing about wine, but I know what I like.'

How often have I listened to this statement pronounced by
inexperienced drinkers. There is, of course, nothing to prevent
you accompanying Pèche Melba with ginger-beer, but I
doubt if there would be many adults to share your taste. The
conventions which combine certain types of wine with certain
types of food are not inflexible laws laid down by irresponsible
people, but the result of experience gained by trial and error
throughout centuries. After all, we want to get the best out of
both food and wine.

You will find, for instance, that red wine with most fish
dishes will give to both a metallic and rather unpleasant taste.
And the freshness and delicacy of a Moselle is, in my opinion,
killed when drunk with red meat.

Taste is the result of educating one's tongue and palate. At
the beginning of our acquaintance with an unaccustomed
flavour our tongue naturally inclines to seek a familiar ingredient. In most cases it is sugar, the most familiar of all
flavours. Remember when you were a child your taste probably veered towards jam, sweet biscuits, cakes and chocolates.
As you grew older the chances are you gravitated to more
savoury flavours—eggs, cheese, ham and bacon, fried fish and
chips.

In one's early experiments in wine-drinking the tongue first
searches for the familiar comfort of sugar. But by the time it
has become more educated, it should be able to reject the

sweetness of cheap wines (not to be compared with the fine balance of natural sweetness and acidity, particularly marked in Sauternes and the late-picked vintages of the Rhine and Moselle), and turn to red wines of more pronounced dryness and character, beginning perhaps with a young Beaujolais, and moving on to the soft fragrance of the greatest Burgundies.

The more opportunities you have for tasting different wines, the more discriminating you will become in your choice. It is not necessary to buy expensive wines to enjoy wine drinking, any more than smoked salmon and foie gras are essential for an epicurean meal.

In most countries wine is intended to be served with food and the principal thing to remember about preparing food to be eaten with wine is to keep it simple. For instance, the ideal meal to set off the nobility of a fine claret is the simplest of hors d'oeuvres (some radishes, a slice of home-made paté and a mushroom salad, for example), followed by a grill accompanied by a lightly dressed salad, or a plainly roast chicken, and ending with cheese. The finer the wine to be served, the less spicy the food should be. This is not to say don't ever serve spicy foods, but marry them to the appropriate wine; a vigorous young Spanish Rioja, or perhaps a Yugoslavian or Dalmatian red wine. The following pages are suggestions to help you to face with confidence the dilemma of marrying wine to food and to help you to ring the changes on your wine-drinking—this is as important as varying your eating habits.

I
Wine

B

Introduction

🎍

Wine is often called a living thing. It is born, develops to a peak of maturity, then slides over the hill towards old age, and finally fades into a shadow of its former substance.

Like the different types of *homo sapiens*, there are many species of vine, though there is only one from which good wine can be made. It is called *Vitis Vinifera*, and is a native of Europe.

The wines of North America, South Africa and Australia are derived from European stock, imported by the first settlers, which have now acquired their own characteristics.

Just over a hundred years ago a tiny beetle-like insect called the phylloxera arrived in Europe in, it is thought, a shipment of fruit from America, and within the next twenty years had decimated almost all the vines all over the continent.

Innumerable experiments were made without success to eradicate the pest, until it began to look as though wine production in Europe must come to an end. Just in time it was discovered that the roots of American vines, though not of the *vinifera* species, were immune to the disease and could be grafted on to European plants. Millions of these vine stocks were at once sent to Europe, and the cuttings were grafted on to the old vine roots. Today all European vines are first grafted on to American roots, and are thus free from a further threat of phylloxera.

Broadly speaking, the best wines come from the poorest soil. It is the type of soil, allied to the climate, which decides the characteristics of a wine.

Could any two wines be more different than the elegant, dry Moselles, and the rich spicy Rheingaus? Yet both are made from the same vine variety, the Riesling. The Pinot grape is used both in Champagne and Burgundy, yet how totally different in quality and style are the wines.

In addition, the weather, that perpetual menace to the tiller of soil, changes the character of every vintage. No two years are ever the same. As a result of these influences some wines attain their maturity more quickly than others.

Wine-making is rather like playing cards. You start out with the same pack, but each time you shuffle the order of your cards invariably presents a different set of problems.

An old countryman once said to me, 'Some men are old at forty-eight. Others are young at eighty-four'. This could equally well apply to wine, and it is what makes the study of wine so fascinating.

ONE

General Information

🦎

While there is no problem in buying wines of accepted vintages from estates of recognized reputation and authenticity, the customer is faced with a perplexing decision when it comes to choosing a wine from an area where many wines, all bearing the same description, are produced by different growers. (See pages 24–7.) It is at this point that the name on the label of the shipper should be noted. Since he is the only contact with both the grower and the retailer his name is the customer's sole guarantee of quality.

A shipper (who may also sometimes be a grower, as in the case of Champagnes, for instance) buys the young wines from the growers which he matures in his cellars until they are ready to be bottled. It is his skilled judgement and selection which bring the good quality wines to the notice of the retailer. If he has established a reputation for knowledge and quality, his name on a label is of paramount importance. A shipper generally specializes only in the wines of the areas from which he ships. (See List of Shippers on pages 139–41.)

A wine merchant will have contacts with many shippers. A good retailer's list will contain, as a rule, wines of many types, price and quality. In the case of large firms some wines may be bottled specially for them. A good and serious retailer is always ready to advise customers on suitable wines for everyday drinking, for special occasions, for drinking within the next few months, and, for those with cellar space, for laying down. This last is a good investment, as most vintage wines (see page 25) increase in value the longer they are kept.

Remember only that while on white wines the accent is generally laid on youth, on red wines it is more often the contrary. The tannin in the latter (contained in the skins and pips of the grapes) gives a long-lasting quality, but at the same time slows up the development so a fine claret may take up to twenty years to reach its highest point of maturity. White wines are usually at their best within five years of their vintage.

Don't be afraid to ask for inexpensive wines in your first adventures in buying. It is here, particularly, that the reliable wine merchant can help, since his experience and reputation will be most likely to give you the best value for your money.

Beware of the door-to-door salesman, who may announce his visit with an 'invitation' card, assuring the prospective buyer that direct sales from producer to consumer will ensure his obtaining wines at bargain prices. In actual fact these prices are usually higher than those of recognized and long-established firms, who work to a very fair profit margin, and who will be prepared to guarantee that when you pull out the cork, the wine which fills your glass corresponds exactly to the details on the label.

You could compare this approach to wine buying with the pursuit of antiques—the bargain which you hope to find in a junk shop as opposed to the guaranteed article from a reputable dealer. Some little while ago, a young wine amateur told me he thought the wines of a world-famous shipper of German wines were too expensive. 'Hey, hey,' I said. 'Before making such a sweeping statement, let's get clear what is meant by expense. What's the difference between a suit you buy for £10, one you buy for £25, and, when you've reached executive level, one you have custom-made for £50?'

'That's easy,' he said. 'To start with, it's better material, and then, there's the cut . . .'

'You needn't go on,' I interrupted. 'You've answered the

question. That is what you pay for when you buy a wine from a reputable firm. It's better material in most cases, and the expertise in making the wine is comparable to the expert cut of a custom-made suit.'

So, deal preferably with a reliable supplier. You are far less likely to be disappointed. Their catalogues usually give a description of the wines they sell. On page 139 you will find a list of the most famous shippers.

When ordering a wine in a restaurant, the wine list may not always give the name of the shipper. If the restaurant is sufficiently large to have a wine waiter, make up your mind how much you are prepared to spend, and ask his advice. You can either build your meal round your wine (if the restaurant is known to have a good cellar) or, if it is famed for its cooking, it is very likely to keep wines suitable for drinking with the food. You should reckon six glasses of wine to a bottle, if filled two-thirds. For four people it is not a bad idea to choose two different wines. This will give more scope to your choice of food, and also give you the opportunity to compare the merits of the wines. In restaurants which specialize in grills, where you may possibly start with a cup of soup and finish with a good piece of cheese, don't be afraid to order wine by the glass or in a carafe.

It happened one evening that I went into such a restaurant, noted for the uniformly good standard of its food. I was tired after a long day, and ordered an artichoke, to be followed by grilled kidneys and bacon. The wine waiter, who knew me, offered his list. Knowing the excellent reputation of the cellar I waved it away, and asked for a half carafe of red Bordeaux. When it came I tasted it, and found it of a quite outstanding quality. I commented on it, and the waiter told me it was precisely the same wine as No. 4 in his list, but the price, without the presentation of bottle and label, was almost half.

Most respectable restaurants supply carafe wine, and there is no discredit in ordering it. It will probably be far better value for the price than the first two or three wines on the list, which may well be something the restaurant is trying to get rid of.

Many years ago my husband took me to a restaurant specializing in the aromatic cooking of the Eastern Mediterranean, about which, at the time, I knew almost nothing. The restaurant was both famous and expensive. After ordering the meal, the wine waiter duly arrived with his *carte*, already open at the page where the finest Bordeaux and Burgundies were listed. My husband gently flipped over the pages till he had found the section dealing modestly with Balkan and Cyprus wines. 'I'm not being mean, darling,' he told me. 'But you'll see that the right thing to drink with this type of food is an unsubtle, full local wine.' He was, of course, perfectly right, as I realized after I had tasted the combination.

I would like to suggest here that you reserve those establishments where music and/or dancing are provided, for occasions when you are intending to drink wine only as a thirst-quencher. To appreciate food and wine requires a quiet ambiance, so that your concentration can do justice to both the skill of the chef, and of the wine maker.

Wine Labels

Wine, while it is not the luxury for the few that it was, is still too expensive to permit extensive preliminary tasting before buying. It is not like cheese, where the salesman helps the customer to make up his mind by offering him a sliver of one or two cheeses to try. To the inexperienced beginner, making a choice of a wine can still be somewhat of a leap in the dark. An elementary knowledge of wine labels can be a help in deciding between the merits of one wine and another.

In France the most important words on a label are '*Appellation Controlée*', which I shall be discussing more fully in the section on French wines.

Bordeaux wines are labelled with the name of the vineyard

followed by the place of origin, a vintage date and usually the name of the proprietor. If the wine has been bottled at the estate, the label should also contain the words '*Mis en bouteille au château*' or '*domaine*' or sometimes '*à la propriété*'. They do not state the name of the grape variety, as in Alsace.

In Burgundy there are very few big estates, and wines are sold under the names of their villages with often the qualification '*Premier Cru*', and the vintage date. The small numbers of large properties are generally called '*clos*' or '*domaine*'. Burgundy labelling is a highly complex question, necessarily inconsistent, as the laws vary from area to area.

Champagne is sold under the name of the shipper who has selected the grapes, made the wine and bottled it. It does not always bear a vintage date. It gives in addition the location of his cellars (Rheims or Epernay) and the style of wine (Brut, Sec, demi-Sec).

The word vintage is a translation of the French *vendange*, meaning harvest. The date on a bottle, therefore, indicates the year in which the wine was made. In other words the date tells you the age of the wine. Since no two years are ever the same, the quality, and even the character, of a wine depends in the first place on the weather conditions of each individual year.

Understandably, the wines from those years whose sequence of sun and rain have occurred at just the right times, are likely to be of higher quality, and consequently to command a higher price. In those countries whose weather follows a similar pattern from year to year (Australia, Argentina, California, for instance), vintages are almost always identical, and the only advantage of a date on a bottle is to tell the age of the wine.

German sparkling wines are labelled under the heading Sekt, and carry the name of the bottler and a brand name. Other sparkling wines state the area of origin, and may add *Méthode Champenoise* if the second fermentation takes place in bottle. This process is explained at the beginning of the chapter on sparkling wines.

The wines of the Loire are classified into vineyard areas, the name of the producer, and a vintage date. The majority of Loire wines are not classified as *Appellation Controlée* but are graded as *Vins Délimités de Qualité Supérieur*. Nevertheless, there are many delightful wines with a style and grace all their own.

The Côtes-du-Rhône usually carry a vineyard name, or a brand name, on their label.

Alsatian wines are labelled with the name of the vine or grape species and, in addition, the name of the producer. The other areas of France sell their wines generally under the regional name, and the name of the vineyard, with the name of the producer, or the proprietor of the vineyard.

When buying German wines, it is important to understand their system of labelling, which, though it appears complicated, nevertheless gives the buyer every detail it is necessary for him to know, e.g., 1967 Winkeler Hasensprung Riesling Auslese. After the date the first word indicates the area, the second the name of the vineyard, the third the type of grape, and the fourth indicates that they were picked after the main harvest. In other words, the wine will have an intensity of colour, bouquet and taste due to the length of time the berries have been allowed to ripen. In addition it will state Erzeuger Abfüllung (bottled at the estate) followed by the name of the owner of the vineyard. In buying wines bearing a brand name such as Hanns Christof Liebfraumilch, Blue Nun, Forellenwein, etc., look at the name of the shipper, who is usually the bottler.

In 1971 the German wine laws were revised and important changes made. In particular, labels will now bear a different method of appellation (see page 92).

Some German wines are described as 'Kabinett'. This usually denotes a special selection, and derives from the period when owners kept their finest wines locked up in a piece of furniture called a *cabinet*, and only brought out a bottle for their most favoured guests.

Fortified wines do not bear a vintage date, with the exception of port, which perhaps two or three times in a decade declares a vintage. Sherries are bottled under the name of their shipper, often bear a brand name, and sometimes the type of blend from which they are made. Other Spanish wines are described either by an analogous French name—as for instance Spanish Burgundy. In the case of vintage Rioja wines the description Casecha (Harvest) or Reserva is followed by the date.

Italian wines, on the other hand, are usually bottled under the name of the shipper. It is particularly important to buy from a reliable firm, in order to make sure that the bottle is correctly labelled, and that the wine conforms to the laws laid down by the *Instituzione del Comitato Nazionale per la Tutelo delle Denominazione di Origine.*

Yugoslavian table wines are generally labelled with the grape variety and the region from which they come as, for instance, Ljutomer Riesling. Hungarian wines are subjected to similar labelling laws.

In Australia most of the wines bear the name of the district, and are generally sold under the name of European vineyards whose type of wine they emulate. South African table wines are usually named by grape variety and, following a trade agreement, do not use *Appellations d'Origine*. (See page 36.) Fortified wines are sold under brand names, since South Africa may not use the words sherry or port on a label.

Californian wines are labelled with the type of grape, and not the area.

STORAGE AND CORKS

If you are lucky enough to have a cellar, store your wines there, in one of the many types of portable bins now on the market.

The principal requirement for the successful storage of wines is to keep them in an even temperature, and a cool one at that: 50° F. (10° C).

In the history of wine, the cork has been certainly the most valuable invention. Before the discovery, at the beginning of the eighteenth century, of this method of allowing wine to age in the bottle, it remained in the cask where it was made. If it was moved from one place to another, in order to exclude the air a finger of oil was run into the bottle—which might be made of glass, leather or pottery—which was then stoppered either with a piece of twisted rag, or with strands of straw.

All still wines should be laid on their side, so that the bottom of the cork is kept wet. This ensures that the cork remains swollen, and makes certain that no air gets to the wine. While wine needs oxygen, the porous substance of the cork provides it with enough. Fortified wines, sparkling wines, brandies (and other spirits) should be stored standing up.

On no account keep your wines in an attic, however dark. Attics are usually subject to too great extremes of temperature. There is nothing worse for wine than being stored in too hot an atmosphere, and an attic, being under the roof, tends to become stuffy and hot in the summer. If you have no cellar, a larder, free from draughts but with a certain amount of ventilation, should prove satisfactory for the storing of small quantities of wine.

BOTTLES

All wines are sensitive to light, which is why most of them are bottled in dark-coloured glass, and why they respond better to being kept undisturbed in the dark. The slim long-necked bottles used for German wines are traditionally coloured brown for Rhine wines and green for Moselle. In France colourless or pale green glass is used for most white wines, and dark green for red. Bordeaux bottles are cylindrical with high shoulders and a sturdy neck. Burgundies appear in a wider bottle, the shoulders tapering towards the neck. Port and sherry bottles have a slight bulge in the middle of the neck. Most brandy bottles are easily recognized by their squat bodies and pronounced shoulders; the glass is usually slightly tinted.

Most liqueurs have their own individually shaped bottles.

The foil-covered necks of sparkling wine bottles are too well-known to be described in any detail.

GLASSES

In the days before corks were invented and glass became cheap enough for wines to be developed in individual bottles, they remained in wooden casks, often till the day they were drunk. In the case of white wines this resulted in the wood oxydizing the wines to the colour of weak tea, instead of the glass-clear, pale golden liquid we are accustomed to see today. They were also full of sediment and other intrusive substances. To hide these imperfections, the practice began of serving wines in coloured glasses. Nowadays, it is almost general practice to serve wine in clear, undecorated glasses, so that its colour and clarity can be seen to the best advantage.

There are many shapes of glasses. If storage space is limited, a tulip or goblet-shaped glass, about 4 inches deep, mounted on a stem, is appropriate for serving most wines. Avoid tumbler shaped glasses. The hand should not (except in the case of brandy) enclose the bowl: first because it hides the colour and clarity of the wine, and, second, because it interferes with the temperature. Hold your glass by the stem.

Never serve champagne, or any sparkling wine, in those abominations supplied by some caterers—a shallow saucer-shaped glass. Use either the long narrow glass called a flute, or a goblet deep enough for the bubbles to spread without brimming over the top.

TEMPERATURE

There is a tendency to overchill white wines, and to overwarm red ones. If you ice a wine, you also refrigerate the bouquet, which is the name given to the burst of perfume which fills the glass before you take your first sip. The better the wine, the better and more intense the bouquet. Wine should charm the nose in preparation for delighting the palate. Professional wine tasters first judge a wine by its 'nose'. So, for white wines, chill them to cellar temperature: 50° F. (10° C.).

Red wines should be drunk at room temperature. Leave the bottle for several hours in a room with a temperature of 65°–70° F. (15°–20° C.). Burgundies and burgundy type wines can be drunk a little cooler than clarets. But never run hot water over a bottle, or stand it near a fire or radiator. Wine is a living thing, and should not be exposed to the shock of violent changes of temperature.

Sherries and other dessert wines, except port, which is best drunk at room temperature, should be drunk at cellar temperature; in other words, cool. Though I know there is a fashion at present to serve sherries iced, and, even, 'on the rocks', I do not believe either of these practices shows the wine to its best advantage. Ice in any wine is an insult to the wine. No wine should be diluted.

Sparkling wines need to be well chilled to bring out their refreshing qualities. It is the low temperature which enhances the sparkle.

Brandies need the warmth of a hand round the glass to release the bouquet. But don't use the enormous balloon glasses in which the wine appears lost at the bottom. A small tulip glass, about 3½ inches long and 2½ inches across the lip, is the best.

THE SERVING OF WINE

In serving any kind of wine, never fill the glass more than half full. If the wine does not have room to 'breathe' you will not get the maximum pleasure from the bouquet. It is a perpetual wonder to me that so many waiters in restaurants invariably pour the wine to within a centimetre of the top of the glass.

If you are serving more than one wine at a meal, start with the youngest. Always serve white wines before red, unless you are planning to end your meal with strawberries, raspberries or ripe fresh peaches, apricots or figs. In this case a Sauternes or a soft Vouvray would be the perfect accompaniment, their fruity sweetness the ideal background for the ripe fruit.

The older a wine, the less it should come into contact with the air before drinking. Generally, the cooler a wine is to be served, the younger it can be drunk. This applies to most white wines, *rosés*, and some light red ones, as, for instance, Beaujolais. Uncork young white wines immediately before serving. Their bouquet will develop in the glass. A red wine between five and ten years old can be uncorked an hour before serving to allow the bouquet to develop, but anything older, and consequently more delicate, should be opened and, if necessary, decanted just before coming to the table. It is only necessary to decant when the wine shows a heavy sediment: the older the wine, the more careful you must be not to disturb the sediment at the bottom of the bottle.

To open the bottle, cut the capsule with a sharp knife, and before drawing the cork wipe any mould off it. After you have drawn the cork, wipe carefully round the inside of the rim. To decant, pour the wine gently and steadily into the decanter until the sediment reaches the neck of the bottle. Then stop.

TWO

Still Wines

🦋

Still wines are either red, white or *rosé*. While you can never make red wine from white grapes, you can, on occasions, make a white wine from black ones. (Champagne is the classic example, since it is largely made from a black grape called the Pinot Noir.)

If you were to press a bunch of white grapes into one glass and a similar bunch of black ones into another, the resulting liquids would be almost identical in colour. The colour in a red wine comes from its skin, so red wines are fermented with their skins and pips while only the juice of white grapes goes into the vats. Generally red wines are drier than white.

The grapes from which white wines are made are capable of producing a juice richer in sugar than black grapes, and it is this alcoholic sweetness which gives to the finest German wines, and also to those of Sauternes, their famous character. Red wines age more slowly than white owing to the tannin contained in the skins and pips, which, although it acts as a preservative (many red wines live to thirty and forty years old, and sometimes fifty plus), also slows up the development.

All wines should look clear and lustrous. As they age their colour changes. In the case of red wines the ruby depth of their youth slowly fades to more russet tones.

In the case of white wines it is the exact reverse. The pale yellow of young wines deepens to gold and sometimes even more intense shades. The fact that in white wines there is no tannin means that, in general, they should be drunk within five years. There are notable exceptions which will be discussed later.

Most still wines are classified as Table Wines. In other words they are intended to be an accompaniment to food.

Note on semi-sparkling wines

A semi-sparkling wine is often described as *'pétillant'* or 'crackling'. The slight prickle is due to a small amount of carbon dioxide present in the wine when it is bottled. In France a pressure of up to two atmospheres is admitted as against five atmospheres in Champagne and Champagne-type wines. (See section on sparkling wines.)

FRANCE

For many hundreds of years French wine and cooking have influenced people all over the world. The language of food is generally accepted to be French, and even in the farthest-flung territories, where the grape has not long since become acquainted with the soil, it is nearly always a French wine type which is planted.

It was France who produced the first sparkling wine, and it was the French who introduced the world to brandy. The most world-famous cooks have been French, and most of the greatest French wine areas are also gastronomic centres.

Wine has been made in France since before the Roman occupation. It was the Romans who taught the uncivilized Gauls the arts of pruning and cultivating their vines. It was the Romans who extended the production from the south and south-west to areas farther north. And it was the Romans who passed on their knowledge to the inheritors of their culture— the Church.

FRANCE

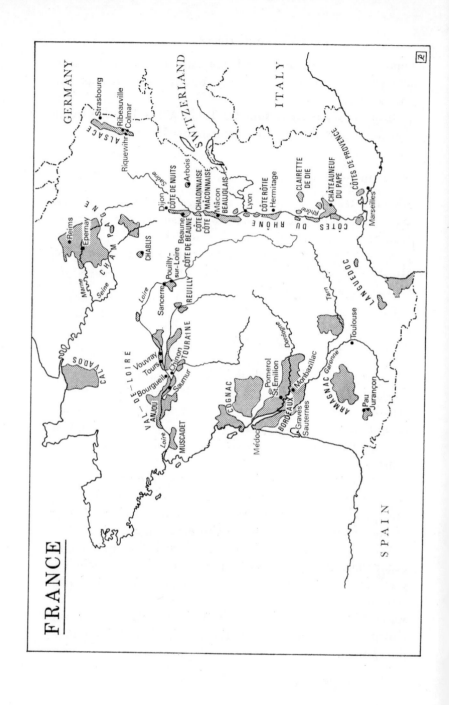

The monks, of necessity, shared their skills with the peasants, so that many of the large estates, particularly in Burgundy, became broken up into small vineyards, and to this day are owned by peasant proprietors.

French wines have been known in England since the twelfth century. In 1152 Henry II, great-grandson of William the Conqueror, married Eleanor of Aquitaine, who brought as her dowry the immense duchy of Aquitaine, which comprised Gascony, Perigord and part of Anjou, with the sovereign rights of Auvergne and the county of Toulouse. During the thirty-five years of his reign Henry spent only thirteen of them in England, and became more powerful than the King of France. He spoke only French, and his French tastes and habits filtered eventually to the other side of the Channel.

The first French wine known to the English was the Clairet de Gascogne, which figured among the merchandise exported at the period from the great port of Bordeaux. It owed its name to its light colour, and was ultimately anglicized to 'claret'.

During the Hundred Years War, Bordeaux continued to trade with England, and throughout the following centuries supplies of claret continued to find their way to the houses of the upper classes.

While the Stuarts reigned French taste again came to the fore, and by the eighteenth century a number of Scottish families had settled in Bordeaux and the surrounding country. Families with names like Johnson, Lawton, Maxwell, Exshaw are a present-day reminder of their pioneering ancestors.

France produces the widest variety of great wines in the world. No other country has such a framework of varying soils and climates, nor uses such a wide range of techniques.

As you will see from the map, if viewed from the air the vineyards of France would be seen roughly as a necklace whose clasp is at Champagne. Following down the eastern boundary are the vineyards of Burgundy, and moving on through the Côtes du Rhône to Châteauneuf du Pape, after a loop to the Côtes de Provence, you would turn westward, north of the Pyrenees, and reach the expansive vineyards of Aquitaine, the ancient name for the vast area of which Bordeaux is the capital. Continuing north-west you would pass over the Charente (the cradle of Cognac) and join the course of the river Loire, where some very attractive wines are produced. Moving eastward you would arrive back at your starting point.

There are two areas outside this circle; those of Alsace and the Jura. The first produces white wines with something of the character of the German Rhine wines, since the vineyards lie along the slopes of the western bank of the river, and the grape varieties are similar—Riesling, Sylvaner and Traminer. The great difference between the character of Alsatian and Rhine wines is that, whereas the greatest of the Rhine wines are those of the late-picked vintages in which the sugar content becomes intensified, the wines of Alsace are always fermented 'dry'— the fermentation continues until there is no sugar left, and the wine is completely dry. Arbois, the principal town of the Jura mountains, is famous for having been the birthplace of Louis Pasteur, and is where he made his famous experiments on the processes of fermentation. The wines are both red and white, and are generally high in alcohol.

Before exploring the principal areas, it is important to know something about the laws of *Appellation d'Origine Controlée.* France is not the only wine-producing country to have evolved a method of protecting her growers, but because wine is the principal agrarian industry (there is scarcely a village, except north of a line drawn from Nantes to the Belgian border, which does not produce some sort of wine) her laws ensure that the customer, too, will be getting the best value for his money.

The *Code du Vin* is a set of regulations which controls and protects the production of wines all over the country. Among the regulations are laws restricting the type of vine which may be planted in each region, the maximum number of hecto-litres allowed to bear the name, and the minimum alcoholic strength. It is, in fact, a guarantee to the customer that the name stated on the label is the correct place of origin for the wine, and that it has been made in accordance with the law. In other words, the stipulated conditions have been complied with.

Besides the wines controlled by *Appellation Controlée*, there are a number which, while better than *vins ordinaires* are not quite worthy of A.O.C. These wines are known as Vins Délimités de Qualité Supérieure, and are mainly found in the areas of the Loire, the Languedoc and Roussillon, the Côtes du Rhône and the Côtes de Provence.

There are also, of course, numbers of small growers whose wines are not controlled either by A.O.C. or V.D.Q.S. These form the basis of the *vins ordinaires* and are also used in the blending of those wines sold under an area or brand name without a vintage date. (See also page 25.) This method of classification, with few deviations, operates all over France.

Burgundy

The second largest wine-producing area in France, Burgundy, whose vineyards were first cultivated by the Romans, has almost as great a reputation for good eating as for good drink-ing. The great cheese dishes, the aromatic beef stews, the *matelotes* of fresh-water fish, the sausages, the famous *jambon persillé* and the even more famous *coq au vin*, were all un-doubtedly invented to complement the qualities of the wines.

The *charcuterie* of the Lyonnais becomes something more than just sausages when accompanied by a crisp young Beaujolais. The much advertised *quenelles de brochet* are un-thinkable without the accompaniment of a dry Pouilly Fuissé. The simplicity of a chicken plainly roasted and basted with fresh country butter is lifted to the realms of great cookery when served with a delicate, scented Volnay.

In the two hundred or so miles between Chablis and Lyon, where the river Saône joins the Rhône, the owners of the vineyards, except in a few cases, do not live in fine houses set in formal parks or gardens surrounded by acres of vines as they do in the Gironde. They are mostly farming people who may have other interests besides cultivating grapes, since the average size of their properties works out at about ten acres.

As one finds also in parts of Germany, many of the most famous vineyards are divided among several owners who each produce a quality of wine totally different from their neighbours. A dozen wines labelled Aloxe-Corton, may come, in fact, from twelve different vineyards, and will consequently vary enormously in quality. It is, therefore, important to look at the name on the label, as growers who produce only small quantities of wine usually find it uneconomical to bottle it themselves. So make sure which are individual estate wines, and which are blended by the bottler.

Generally a single name denotes a better-quality wine than a hyphenated one. The name of the village, e.g. Aloxe, is stated before that of the vineyard, e.g. Corton, so a bottle labelled Corton should contain a superior wine to a bottle labelled Aloxe-Corton because it comes from a specific vineyard. This applies similarly to Musigny, the vineyard stretching along the slope above the beautiful medieval château of Clos de Vougeot, formerly a Cistercian monastery, and controlled by the village of Chambolle. The vineyards of Romanée are planted around Vosne; Nuits, whose best-known vineyard is, of course, St Georges, lies adjacent to Gevrey, known under the name of its greatest vineyard, Chambertin.

Small vineyards are not named but use instead the description *premier cru* on their label as may also the villages themselves. The outstanding vineyards may be described as *Grand Crus* or *Tête de Cuvée*.

The wines of Burgundy are some of the most noble in

France. They are both red and white, are always dry, and are nearly all characterized by a beautiful scent and flavour.

The main areas are Chablis, famous for its dry white wines of exceptional finesse, and Côte d'Or, incorporating Côte de Nuits and Côte de Beaune. They include some of the most aristocratic names in wine records, the first containing Gevrey-Chambertin, Morey St Denis, Chambolle-Musigny, Clos de Vougeot, Vosne-Romanée and Nuits St Georges; the second Aloxe-Corton, Beaune, Pommard, Volnay, Santenay, Corton-Charlemagne, Meursault and Puligny-Montrachet. The last three are perhaps the princes of French white wines, while Romanée-Conti, Richebourg, La Tache and Chambertin are usually considered the patricians of the red.

The centre of the Burgundian wine trade is indisputably at Beaune, not only because of its outstanding vineyards, but because the town is dominated by the beautiful buildings of the Hospices de Beaune, a hospital and home for old people, founded in the fifteenth century, and owning some of the finest vineyards in the vicinity, mostly donated by local philanthropists. Each year, after the vintage, a public auction is held in the courtyard of the hospital and the wines are sold according to tradition. The wines of Beaune are generally lighter in character than most of the other Burgundies.

Following the course of the river Saône on its journey to the south, we pass through the Côte Chalonnaise. The river bends at Chalon-sur-Saône on its way to the Côte Mâconnais, where we find Pouilly Fuissé, the finest white wine of southern Burgundy.

Beaujolais

Continuing south, we are at once in the Beaujolais, whose light and refreshing young red wines are drunk all over the world. There is also a small quantity of *rosé* produced in the Beaujolais area. The vineyards follow in quick succession, Moulin-à-Vent,

Fleurie, Morgon and Brouilly, and a few miles farther on are the outskirts of Lyon, the second most important city in France. Besides being the centre of the silk industry, its busy streets contain numberless restaurants all offering versions of the famous *charcuterie*, endless forms of pork cookery, and the renowned pike *quenelles*. Here it is that the Saône meets the Rhône, an important river flowing south from its source in Switzerland.

Côtes du Rhône

Rhône wines are similar in type to Burgundies, though in general they are fuller, have less subtlety, and are darker in colour.

Many of the red wines contain the Syrah grape, said to have been brought originally from the Middle East by the Crusaders. It gives a highly individual flavour to the wine, warm, generous and pleasant.

The best-known areas are Château Grillet, producing a dry, rich white wine, Côte Rotie, whose wines have a very recognizable character, somewhere between a Burgundy and a Bordeaux. Hermitage, made from the Syrah grape growing in a mixture of granite and chalky soil, results in big long-living wines with a glowing purple reflection in their depths, an intense bouquet, and a velvety quality in maturity. The small amount of white wine made has its own distinctive fruity taste. The most famous of all the high-quality red wines of the Côtes du Rhône is, of course Châteauneuf du Pape. Since it makes over a million and a half gallons of wine a year its reputation has tended to overshadow its neighbours. The wines are firm and fresh with a fine bouquet.

Provence

The moment one leaves the steep hills bordering the Rhône valley one is in the golden country of Provence, and the country of herb-flavoured grills, of *brandade de morue* (the famous dish of salt cod creamed with olive oil and milk), of anchovies and olives, of young fresh vegetables and fruits warm from the sun.

Although Provence is usually associated with *rosé* wines, a number of red, full-bodied and powerful wines are made, as befits the aromatic and strongly-flavoured food. From the Languedoc, to the west of Provence, comes the best known of all French *rosé* wines, Tavel. In colour it inclines towards the brownish tones of those wines known as 'onion-skin'. In character the accent is on youth, and the wines should not be kept above three years.

In the south of the Languedoc the vines grow in great profusion. The best area is that of Rousillon, producing lively and thirst-quenching wines from the slopes known as Corbières de Rousillon. As we continue on our journey to the west the food becomes richer, since goose fat or pork lard is substituted for the olive oil of Provence and the fresh butter of Burgundy. Geese, pork or ducks are preserved in their own thick white fat, and form the basis of most of the spicy local cookery. Red peppers, spicy sausages and smoky hams do not invite an accompaniment of subtly-flavoured wines. The local wines are mostly rustic in style and are both red and white. Jurançon, whose vines grow along the foothills of the Pyrenees near the principal city of Pau, produces golden sweet wines with a unique and rather heady, flowery scent.

It is only as we pass through the Dordogne that we begin to prepare ourselves for the splendours of the Bordelais, since the wines, though they cannot be compared in quality have, nevertheless, something of the same characteristics. There is one white wine, whose full, rich sweetness is somewhat similar to Sauternes. This is Monbazillac, in good years producing a wine which, if allowed to age, can achieve real distinction.

Bordeaux

Already a port in the time of the Romans, the city of Bordeaux flourished until the fourth century, when it passed through several hundred dark years until Henry II married Eleanor of Aquitaine in 1152. From then onwards, although many other industries were started, the wine trade always came first and has remained so till today.

The vineyards which come under the heading of Bordeaux are the most extensive in France, and the wines are, by a long way, the most varied in type and character. They are both white and red. Broadly speaking, the principal red wine areas lie to the north and east of the city, and the white wines to the south. Nearly all the finest wines are produced from vineyards planted along the banks of the river Garonne, which, a few miles to the north of the city, joins the Dordogne and becomes the Gironde flowing towards its outlet in the Bay of Biscay.

The proximity of Bordeaux to the sea has resulted in a number of regional fish dishes, the most notable being the *Lamproie aux poireaux et au vin rouge* (one of the rare instances in which fish is cooked successfully in red wine), *les langoustines au Cognac* (a variation of *homard à l'Americaine*), and *Grillade d'alose*, only possible in the spring when the shad swim down the river towards the sea. When caught they are simply grilled over vinewood and sprinkled with chopped shallot before serving. The other famous regional dishes are *Cèpes à la Bordelaise*, the large spongy green mushrooms found in the woods of the locality and stewed in olive oil with garlic and parsley, and *Entrecôte à la Bordelaise*. The latter is traditionally grilled over the glowing embers of vinewood, and served with marrow spread over the top surface, which is then sprinkled with chopped parsley and shallots.

Most of the food is designed to act as a background to the wines and, even at vintage banquets, the food is usually of an intentional simplicity. It is only at the end that the skill and

42

artistry of the *chef* are allowed to run riot in the composition of the sweet dishes.

All Bordeaux wines are at their best with food. The reds are mostly dry, often with a scent and taste of cedar. They are rarely 'fruity', except around St Emilion and Pomerol, when they have a warmth of flavour which brings with it a certain velvety and 'grapey' quality. The white wines of the Sauternes and the Graves, on the other hand, tend to be medium to sweet. Until recently even the local oysters used to be accompanied by Cérons, a white wine from a district adjoining Barsac, and though the wines are less sweet than the typical Barsacs, they are still sweeter than those we are accustomed nowadays to serve with shellfish.

In 1855, on the occasion of the Great Exhibition in Paris, a classification was made of the best wines of Bordeaux in order of quality. Sixty-two wines were chosen and graded into five growths or *Crus*. They are known as the classed growths or *Crus Classés*. With the exception of one they are all red wines of the Médoc, the peninsula running north from Bordeaux to the Pointe de Grave. The exception is Château Haut Brion, a red Graves of such superlative quality that it was included in the list, and is one of the four first growths. A growth is not a grade. It is a translation of the word *cru*, which derives from the verb *croître*, to grow (in the sense of development).

The objection to this classification is that it is incomplete, since it does not include any wines from St Emilion or Pomerol (on the opposite side of the river), though it gave a separate classification for Sauternes. In 1855 only one Sauternes, Château d'Yquem, was classed as a *Premier Grand Cru*, eleven were classed *Premiers Crus*, and twelve as *Second Crus*. The advantage of these classifications is that they give an indication of the sort of quality you may expect.

After the *Crus Classés* come the *Crus Bourgeois*, graded into *Crus Exceptionnels*, *Crus Bourgeois Superieurs* and *Crus Bourgeois*. Among the two thousand or so estates, the *Crus Bourgeois* offer the best value for money. The prices of most of the great classified growths are beyond the reach of most people's pockets, but with careful buying, a cellar of interesting and excellent-quality wines can be assembled from among these lesser growths. The Médoc offers hundreds of wines from areas such as Listrac, Soussans, Arcins, St Laurent, Avensan and Labarde in the Haut Médoc, and the areas north of St Estephe in the Bas Médoc.

On the opposite side of the river the slopes of St Emilion and its neighbouring estates at Pomerol contain some of the oldest names in French history. Indeed, St Emilion is claimed to be the oldest town in France. The poet Ausonius, in the third century, lived in a villa just outside the city and sang the glories of the green valley. Louis XIV called the wines of St Emilion 'the nectar of the Gods', and their generous bouquet, their roundness of flavour and their deep ruby colour make them perhaps easier to appreciate than the more austere nobility of the great Médoc growths. A number of vineyards in the Côtes de Fronsac, Côtes de Bourg, and Côtes de Blaye, while not of the fullness and warmth of St Emilion, produce wines capable of admirably complementing a meal.

The city of Bordeaux stands in the centre of the Graves, an area more famous for its white wines than its red. This is curious, as most of the white wines are generally uninteresting, sweetish and mediocre, while many of the red wines achieve real distinction. They have more body and, in youth, a certain hardness, than the Médocs, but even in bad years they are never less than good. A classification of the best was made in 1959, and comprises six white and seven red.

On the opposite side of the river are the Premières Côtes de Bordeaux, also making white and red wines. The wines used to be sweet, but as the general taste now demands drier wines, many of the growers are producing agreeable inexpensive wines in this style.

Adjoining the Graves on its southern boundary is the district of Sauternes, the area which produces the most rich, suave, almost unctuous, white wines in the whole of France.

The grapes develop a valuable mould called *botrytis cinera*, which attacks them late in the autumn. As in the late-picked vintages of Germany, the mould shrivels the skins of the grapes while reducing the amount of water in the berries, so that the proportion of sugar is intensified. The mould does not develop on every bunch of grapes, so a vineyard may have to be picked over half a dozen or so times. For this reason true Sauternes are always expensive. The most famous Sauternes is, of course, Château d'Yquem. Within the area are also the *communes* of Preignac, Bommes, Fargues and Barsac, all producing similar wines, though Barsac, because of its particularly distinctive character, has been accorded an *Appellation Controlée* of its own.

Sauternes were served sometimes with fish. I think most people today would agree that the wines show up best against the natural sweetness of soft fruit, or desserts in which fruit is an ingredient.

Across the river lie the vineyards of the Entre Deux Mers, a large area producing light clean white wines. There are no outstanding growths, but the best wines are made at Loupiac and Ste-Croix-du-Mont.

Leaving Bordeaux the road branches north through Cognac, which we will discuss under the heading of distilled wines. Its vineyards are planted along the west bank of the river Charente, almost as well known for its dairy and vegetal produce.

Loire

About a hundred miles farther north are the vineyards of the Loire, whose six hundred miles length make it the longest river in France. It empties itself into the Atlantic at Nantes, where fishing is an important industry, and the dry crisp white wines marry incomparably with the many varieties of sea food. From the villages between Saumur and Tours come little cream cheeses called *cremets*, eaten with sugar as a dessert, and even more exquisite when accompanied by a soft Vouvray. *Rillettes de porc*, a sort of potted pork, is a favourite hors d'oeuvre, and many versions of chicken and duck cookery combine admirably with the red wines of Chinon and Bourgueil. There are none of the robust beef stews and substantial *charcuterie* of the Burgundians in this cool lyrical climate, whose poplar-fringed landscapes always remind me of a painting by Corot. Like the wines, the food is light in character. The wines are chiefly white and *rosé*. The best are graceful, dry and wonderfully refreshing. Around Chinon some excellent red wine is made, and in the areas of Saumur and Vouvray a considerable amount of sparkling and semi-sparkling wine is also produced. The most distinguished of the white wines are Sancerre, Pouilly Fumé, and Muscadet, which are all characterized by an elegant dry crispness, and a delightfully scented bouquet. Vouvray is a case apart, since its best wines are sweet, with an ingratiating softness.

Anjou is renowned for its *rosé* wines, firm and refreshing. This area also produces an agreeable sweet white wine, Bonnezeaux.

We have now reached the end of our circular tour of French vineyards, and I cannot do better than close the clasp with a comment on the still wines of Champagne (the sparkling wines of Champagne are discussed in another chapter), whose vines are among the oldest in the country. The still wines are known as Vins Natures de Champagne. The best is *Bouzy rouge*, a delicate wine with something of the finesse of a light Burgundy, which can provide most enjoyable drinking. *Blanc de blancs* can also make excellent drinking with spring and summer food.

Alsace

Unlike the wines of other French vineyard areas, those of Alsace do not generally carry the names of their localities of origin, but the names of the vine or grape species from which they are made. They may or may not carry the name of their producer, so in choosing a wine, therefore, it is important to make sure that the label does bear, not only the name of an established and reputable producer, but also the growth. In this way you can be sure of a standard of quality, similar to the system in Champagne.

Practically all Alsatian wines are white and are bottled, like the wines of the Moselle, in tall, slender, dark green glass bottles.

They are made chiefly from Sylvaner, Riesling, Traminer and Gewürztraminer grapes. Their character is light, crisp and fresh with a fine bouquet. Curiously enough, besides being an ideal accompaniment for most kinds of *charcuterie* and fish, they are excellent with more spicy foods. In fact, the only wine I have ever drunk successfully with a curry was an Alsatian Gewurztraminer. Its dry and aromatic nature stood up quite extraordinarily against the pungent food.

Jura

Although compared to other districts the Jura does not produce large quantities of wine, from the steep slopes of the mountains ranging between Burgundy and the Swiss border come some curious and interesting wines. The two most striking are the *vins jaunes*, and the *vins de paille*. Both are made from grapes grown in no other part of France and, as their names imply, both are white.

The *vins jaune* are fermented for several weeks, and after being transferred to casks, remain there for a minimum period of six years. During this time a grey film forms on the top of the wine, like the *flor* which forms on sherry. A certain amount of wine evaporates, and is never replaced, giving the wine a strong flavour something like a light sherry, though the wine is not fortified.

Vins de paille, on the contrary, are sweet and best drunk with dessert. Their name comes from the straw mats on which the grapes are laid to dry for two or three months before being pressed. The fermentation takes a long time because of the richness of sugar in the grapes, and must ferment out to 15 per cent alcohol, which makes them too heavy as a table wine.

Corsica

The island of Corsica is shaped something like a closed fist, with the index finger pointing towards the French coast.

Until a comparatively short time ago, the wine industry in Corsica could be best described as haphazard. The grapes grew rampantly in the warm Italianate climate, were generally uncared for, and were vinified more by luck than judgement. They were red, white and *rosé* and inclined to be fiery.

Within the last ten years a number of Frenchmen from Algiers have settled in Corsica, and have not only planted new vines, but are using their experience and expertise to establish a properly balanced wine industry. The wines are now vigorous and robust, unexpectedly high in alcohol, and make agreeable drinking with the local highly seasoned food.

Corsican specialities are young kid roasted with mountain herbs, highly spiced and smoked *charcuterie*, cream cheeses made from goats' milk, and a dessert based on chestnut flour flavoured with citron.

The best wines come from the finger-like peninsula called Cap Corse. Patrimonio Rosé, produced near Bastia, is the most reputed.

GERMANY
(*N.B.*—First see Postscript on page 92.)

The vineyards of Germany are claimed to be the most northerly in the world, so the production of wine presents some quite special problems.

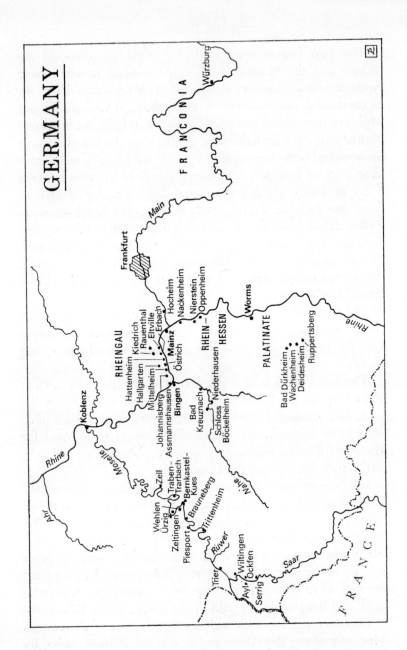

GERMANY

FRANCONIA

Würzburg

Main

Frankfurt

RHEINGAU

Hattenheim
Hallgarten
Mittelheim
Kiedrich
Rauenthal
Eltville
Erbach
Hocheim
Nackenheim
Nierstein
Oppenheim

Mainz
Östrich

RHEIN — HESSEN

Worms

PALATINATE

Bad Dürkheim
Wachenheim
Deidesheim
Ruppertsberg

Johannisberg
Assmannshausen
Bingen

Bad
Kreuznach

Schloss
Böckelheim
Niederhausen

Koblenz

Rhine

Moselle

Rhine

Ahr

Zell
Traben-
Trarbach
Bernkastel-
Kues
Wehlen
Ürzig
Zeltingen
Piesport
Brauneberg
Trittenheim

Nahe

Ruwer

Trier
Ayl
Serrig
Wiltingen
Ockfen
Saar

FRANCE

D

The two largest wine-producing areas are those of the Rhine and the Moselle. Although Germany is not a large wine-producing country compared with France or Italy, she is supreme as the producer of white wines, whose quality and style are unmatched anywhere in the world. She is, however, fundamentally a beer-drinking country (at the last assessment of wine and beer consumption in 1969, one hundred and thirty-five litres of beer were consumed per head as against fifteen litres of wine), and her substantial food is better adapted to beer than to wine. Consequently many of her finest wines are better drunk away from the dining-table. There is, nevertheless, one type of cooking which marries incomparably with Rhine wines. This is the slow stewing of all kinds of game. Venison, hare, pheasant and wild boar are the principal kinds found in Germany.

The wines of the Moselle, on the other hand, are at their best when combined with fish dishes, chicken and veal. Their delicate freshness is exactly right with what I should call 'spring food'.

The name Hock is an anglicization of Hochheim, a town at the elbow of the Rhine, where the Main flows in from the east. The wines of Hochheim were reputed to be much liked by Queen Victoria, who allowed her name to be used for the most famous vineyard. The story goes that she said, 'A little Hock keeps away the Doc'.

It is believed that wine has been made in Germany since the beginning of the Christian era. The earliest known bottle of wine in the world was found in a Roman sarcophagus near Speyer in the Palatinate (see page 53) and, from coins unearthed in the same tomb, it has been possible to date the wine exactly to the year A.D. 300. Having been covered with a thick layer of oil to insulate it from the air the wine has not evaporated, and has remained liquid in the bottle.

Certainly the Romans laid the foundations of the famous vineyards along the Rhine and it was the Romans who, by reason of their law of inheritance which decreed that estates must be left to descendants in equal shares, dissected them into the snippets which today form the majority of vineyards along the banks of the Rhine and Moselle. From this *force majeure* numbers of small growers in the secondary areas, doubtless having neither the capital nor the facilities to transform such small amounts of grapes into wine, began to sell their crops to larger producers, who displayed their skill by blending the several musts into harmonious wines, characteristic and typical of their area. The difference between these wines and those from a single estate is that, while most wines blended by a reputable shipper bear a vintage date, their quality and style do not vary from one year to another, since the art of the wine-maker ensures a continuity of balance, whereas an estate wine must contain only grapes from its own vineyard and is primarily dependent on the weather for both its quality and quantity.

German wines can, therefore, be divided into two main categories: wines blended from a region by the shipper, and authentic bottlings from an estate. In good years grapes in this second category are graded.

After the main vintages certain bunches are left on the vines to ripen further. It follows that the wines made from these grapes are richer in sugar and, consequently, higher in alcohol. From these bunches individual berries may be selected to mellow still more. As with Sauternes, the mould called *botrytis cinera* covers the grapes, those which have dried to the consistency of a raisin being set aside for the finest and sweetest wines.

These gradings appear always on the label.

Spätlese	= late picked
Auslese	= selected bunches
Beerenauslese	= selected berries
Trockenbeerenauslese	= selected *botrytis*-covered over-ripe berries

The principal grape used in German wine production is the Riesling. In the Rheinhessen and the Palatinate, Sylvaner, and a cross between the Riesling and Sylvaner called Müller-Thurgau (after its inventor), are grown.

Along the steep banks of the Moselle the grapes are individually staked, and on the more gradual slopes of the Rhine they are trained on wires, as in France. The vines in this bleak and austere soil need all the sun they can get, so they are planted where they are most likely to receive not only the maximum amount of sunshine, but the maximum reflection of the sun off the water. This slow ripening results in wines of a delicious freshness, their sweetness edged with a subtle acidity obtained by no other means, and therein lies their charm. In this unamiable climate the vintage takes place at least a month later than in most of the other European countries, and it often happens that the last grapes are harvested after the first frosts.

In years when the autumn is prolonged into the beginning of December, it is sometimes possible to make an Eiswein. For this the grapes must be picked when the frost is not only on the berries, but has also frozen the juice. The grapes must be pressed while the juice is still frozen. The resulting wine has a concentrated sweetness even more intense than a Trocken-beerenauslese.

After the Roman era, control of the vineyards was assumed by the Church, that pillar of the Middle Ages, and many of the finest vineyards are still in the possession of religious bodies.

The great majority of German wines are white. Red wines are made in the Ahr valley, a northern tributary of the Rhine, in parts of the Palatinate, at Assmanshaussen in the Rheingau, and around Württemberg, but they cannot be compared with the red wines of France, Italy or Spain, and are, as a rule, not sold outside the country.

Rhine

The major wine-producing areas are the Rheingau, the home of the greatest estates. The wines are the aristocrats of German wine production. Made from Riesling grapes they are firm and rich, with great nobility and an unmistakable intensity of flavour. If you look at a map, it is easy to see why the Rheingau has acquired its reputation. The grapes grow on the slopes of hills facing south towards the river, so that they benefit from uninterrupted sunshine.

Turning south round the elbow of the Rhine at Mainz we come to the Rheinhessen, which extends as far as Worms. The wines made chiefly from the Sylvaner grape, except around Nierstein where a proportion of Riesling grapes are grown, are softer, rounder and quicker to develop than the wines of the Rheingau. Though they never attain the distinction and breed of the Rheingau wines they are nevertheless attractive, and make pleasant drinking. It is in this area that the famous Liebfraumilch was first made. Its production was formerly restricted to the vines growing around the Church of our Lady (Liebfrauenstift) at Worms. But, as the German wine law now stands, the name may be used to describe an agreeable wine from almost any Rhine district. To make sure that you buy a brand from the original district, it is important to look at the name of the shipper. The most famous and reliable of these are Deinhard & Co., Hallgarten, Langenbach, Sichel and Valckenberg.

Following the course of the Rhine, we come to the Palatinate, one of the prettiest stretches of the river, for almost as many orchards are planted as vineyards, and the half-timbered houses, gay with brightly-filled window-boxes and decorated with painted designs on their steep gables, line either side of the narrow cobbled streets.

The Riesling and Traminer grapes grown on the slopes of the Haardt mountains produce, at their best, wines whose sweetness and fine bouquet rival those of the Rheingau.

Between the Rhine and the Moselle flows the Nahe which, although geographically a tributary of the Rhine, gives to its wines some of the characteristics of both rivers. Though lighter than those of the Rheingau, they yet have something of their spiciness, while at the same time their flowery bouquet recalls the feminine crispness of the Moselle.

There is a group of other vineyards which start at the river Main, another tributary of the Rhine, which it joins at Mainz. The only one with which we need concern ourselves comes from the area called Franconia. These wines are traditionally bottled in a flask-shaped bottle called a *Bocksbeutel*. It can be assumed that the origin of these bottles was the leather wine skin of the Middle Ages, when the flattened sides prevented the bottle from rolling against either the hip of its owner, or against the rump of his horse.

Franconian wines, though made predominantly from the Sylvaner grape, have an earthy dryness, quite different in character from any other German wine. The most famous is the Würzburger Steinwein, made from grapes grown on the slopes overlooking the beautiful city of Würzburg, noted for its baroque architecture which includes the Residenz, the bishop's palace designed in 1719 by Balthasar Neumann and containing the celebrated painted ceilings by Tiepolo. The collection of sculpture by Tilman Riemenschneider, the sixteenth-century carver, is housed in a palace-cum-fortress built high above the city, with magnificent views across the vineyards. The wines' stony austerity is admirably complemented by any fish dish cooked *au bleu*, or baked in the oven and served with a sauce in which milk or cream do not figure. They are excellent too with mild cheeses such as Edam or Gruyère.

Moselle

The Moselle is divided into three parts, the Lower, the Middle and the Upper. The second reach includes the wines of two tributaries, the Saar and the Ruwer. The wines of the Lower Moselle (the part which converges with the Rhine at Koblenz) lack some of the distinction of the great wines of the Moselle (and they can be very great indeed), which belong to the middle stretch of the river.

The wines, green-gold in colour, are characterized by an extreme delicacy, an incomparable freshness, and an intense flowery bouquet. The grapes grow on the steep slopes of the river and are of one variety, the Riesling. The twisting and winding river softens the austerity of the rocky hillsides whose menacing appearance is broken by picturesque villages dotted along either bank. The vines grow on narrow terraces of broken-up slabs of slate held by the thinnest of soil. Although at certain points a primitive system of winch has been installed, the greater proportion of viticultural equipment is carried on foot up the almost precipitous ascents. It follows that the grapes at vintage time are carried down by the same means, and it is no more than usual to see a man carrying a load of sixty to a hundred pounds of ripe grapes on his back.

The vineyards of the Middle Moselle start at Trier, reputed to be the oldest city in Germany (and still showing several well-preserved examples of the Roman occupation). Also famous as the birthplace of Karl Marx, and the frontier between Germany and Luxembourg, it follows the curves of the river as far as Reil, a small village whose vines, planted high in the hills, look down on the water. All the most outstanding wines come from these few miles of snaking bends.

The slate which composes the vineyards varies in density. On the Doktorberg, where the vines of the most famous of all Moselle vineyards grow, there are thirty metres of slate between the vineyard and the seventeenth-century cellar belonging to Deinhard, the majority owner, carved out of the rock beneath it. It is just this depth of slate in which the vines are rooted which gives to the wine its unique quality and breed, for it holds both moisture and heat. In this geographical phenomenon linked by its alliance with the Riesling grape, lies the secret of all the Middle Moselle wines. In spite of their infinite variety they all have in common an elegance and a finesse which stamps them inimitably. The wines of the Saar have, as one might expect, many of the characteristics of the Moselle, though they are generally more spicy, crisp and often slower to age.

The Ruwer wines are light and tend to be drier, with a higher degree of acidity. The best vineyards of the Upper Moselle are planted on the slopes opposite Luxembourg. As the soil is chalk and not slate, the wines have a quite different character from those of the Middle Moselle. Though they are light, they have a certain charm and worth, but they cannot in any way compete with the wines of the central portion of the river.

ITALY

It is not difficult to understand why Italy is the largest wine-producing country in the world. From the north to the south the vine has triumphantly appropriated the soil. It sprawls rampantly over pergolas, it climbs around trees, it festoons terraces, it shares fields with other produce . . . and sometimes it is harnessed in neat rows. Nearly always the grapes are large and luscious. This casual method of cultivation results, as one might expect, in wines ranging in quality from the fine-scented growths of Piedmont, Lombardy and Tuscany, to the standardized cheap products bearing only the name of a co-operative.

A number of growers have formed themselves into *consorzii*, and make their wines according to a set of rules rather like the *Appellation Controlée*. The members of the *consorzii* hold the right to add a crest on their labels as a sign of guarantee and the words *controllato* and *garantito*. The best known is the black cock affixed to *Chianti Classico*. The classic cheese-enriched

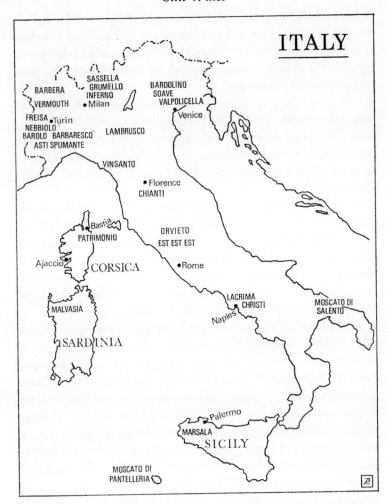

ITALY

BARBERA
VERMOUTH
SASSELLA
GRUMELLO
INFERNO
• Milan
BARDOLINO
SOAVE
VALPOLICELLA
FREISA • Turin
NEBBIOLO
BAROLO BARBARESCO
ASTI SPUMANTE
LAMBRUSCO
• Venice

VINSANTO

• Florence
CHIANTI

Bastia
PATRIMONIO
ORVIETO
EST EST EST

Ajaccio
CORSICA
• Rome

MALVASIA
LACRIMA
CHRISTI
Naples
MOSCATO DI
SALENTO

SARDINIA

• Palermo
MARSALA
SICILY

MOSCATO DI
PANTELLERIA

pastas, the sauces based on tomatoes and red wine, the meat stews aromatized with mountain herbs all seem to call for the exuberant red wines of the mountainous districts in the north.

The white wines are traditionally drunk with the many varieties of fish, fried to a crusty crispness in olive oil, as well as the milder types of *charcuterie* and fresh cheeses. One of the best-

57

known white wines is Orvieto, a delightful summer drink. It is one of the most pleasant of Italian wines, and is either sweet or dry. Soave, a dry white wine from Verona, with a light and agreeable bouquet, is characterized, as its name implies, by a smoothness on the tongue.

One of the best slow-maturing red wines is Barolo, a robust wine from Piedmont. From the same district comes Barbaresco, with a marked depth and a pungent after-taste. Both these wines make an excellent accompaniment to country-type food, especially that which includes the local strong earthy-flavoured mushrooms.

In the north of the Lombardy plains a lightly sparkling wine, called Grumello, is made, often with an unexpected delicacy and, a little farther to the south, the luxuriant vineyards of Frecciarossa produce red, white and *rosé* wines. The white wine in particular is often exceptionally crisp and fragrant. Valpolicella, a wine made in various qualities, is at its best rich and fruity, with sometimes a slight prickly taste.

The hills of Tuscany provide the grapes for the best known of all Italian wines, if only from their easily recognizable straw-covered flasks. I mean, of course, Chianti. It can be fine and beautifully perfumed. It can be rough and characterless. There are some Chiantis produced in a handful of estates (Brolio is the largest and most widely known) which have the best qualities of the finest wines. They are not sold in the traditional flask, but in narrow brown bottles. Owing to their complicated method of vinification, they are not, as a rule, sold until they are at least seven or eight years old, and they are relatively expensive. But they make distinguished and honourable drinking.

The island of Sardinia is veined with mountains and vines. Lying as it does in the warm waters of the Mediterranean, the bulk of the wines tend to have the alcoholic strength of the fortified wines of Sicily and Spain. They are generally sweet and strong, without great breed.

SPAIN

The oenological reputation of Spain, without any doubt, has been founded on the few square miles of vineyards planted in the south-west corner of the country producing the fortified wine known as Sherry, and the other area in the north in which grow the trees responsible for providing the bark used in the manufacture of corks.

The world-wide renown of Sherry has rather eclipsed the wines made in other areas. Nevertheless, fortified dessert wines are produced in Tarragona and Malaga, and a number of table wines capable of standing up to spicy olive-flavoured food are made in other districts.

Spain also makes wines of French types bearing appropriate names on the labels like Chablis, Sauternes, Burgundy, etc. The most important table wine is Rioja, made from grapes growing along the dusty, pale banks of the river Ebro, in the ancient kingdom of Castile. The climate is somewhat similar to Bordeaux, temperate winters with little or no snow, and long hot summers and autumns. The best wines are round and warm with a distinctive aromatic perfume, and are the best value for money of almost any wine in the world. Valdepeñas is also a good buy. The wines are sound, the reds strong and the whites dry. In the summer the red wine is often iced and served mixed with orange or lemon juice and sugar. It makes a most refreshing and imaginative drink called locally Sangria. Spanish food is nearly always redolent of olives, tomatoes, pimentos and garlic. The staple dishes are mainly based on fish (of which there are innumerable and unfamiliar kinds), heavily spiced sausages and rice. The food often brings a breath of Arabian taste, a reminder of the epoch when Spain was influenced by Moorish culture.

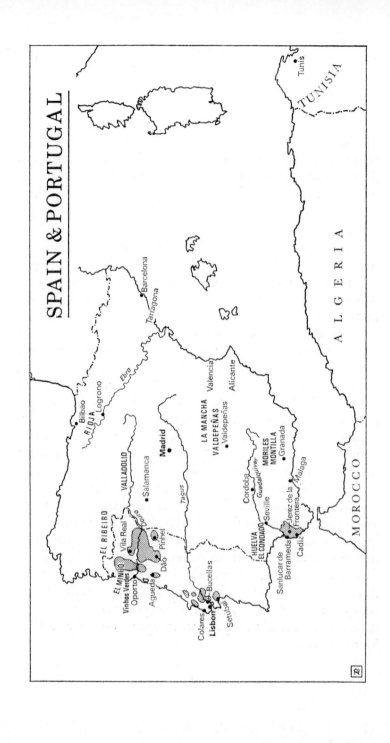

PORTUGAL

As Spain brings first to mind Sherry, so Portugal has been principally associated with Port. Recently, however, the name of Portugal has become synonymous also with the pink prickly wine sold under the name of Mateus rosé.

Between Port and Rosé, from countless areas of vines, there is a number of table wines which achieve both excellence and distinction.

The greatest number of Portuguese wines come under the category of *Vinhos Maduros*—mature wines. The majority are red, and are made in the crumbling, rocky country bordering the river Douro, and in Dão, the valley of the beautiful and wild mountainous area lying to the south of the river. The quality of these wines is consistently good. South in the province of Estramadura, of which Lisbon is the capital, the grapes grow on the low cliffs facing the sea. Here one finds Calares, a dark red wine, often with a peculiar smoky taste. It is slow to develop, and may be left several years in the cask before bottling. Calares also produces a white wine.

The best white wines are mainly dry and come from Bucelas, north of Lisbon, Dão and Douro, from where they may be sold direct from the cask.

The light, sharp, slightly prickly wines called *Vinhos Verdes* (Green Wines) are made in the most northerly part of the country. They are essentially wines for summer drinking as, containing only a low amount of alcohol, they are refreshing, and should be drunk as young as possible. Chilled to the point of misting the glass, they are especially delicious as an accompaniment to all kinds of shellfish, and fish cooked without rich sauces. They also make a most agreeable aperitif in hot weather.

These wines should bear on their label an equivalent of *Appellation d'Origine*, although they do not as a rule carry a vintage date.

AUSTRIA

The most famous wine exported from Austria is marketed under the somewhat inelegant name of Schluck (meaning to gulp or swallow).

It is indeed the sort of fresh, slightly prickly wine which one finds served in carafe in every Viennese café. Made from the Sylvaner grape it is, though less delicate than its German equivalent, none the less a clean, flowery and thirst-quenching drink, the sort of refreshment perhaps enjoyed by Mozart and Schubert and, later, the Strausses, in the cool dark cafés, and by Beethoven, after his long walks through the wooded slopes of the Grinzing hills lying above the city. Wine has been made in Austria since the days of the Romans, and there is no doubt that the early traditions were handed down via the Church to those princely landowners, whose estates often comprised several villages. Nowadays it is rare to find estate bottled wine outside Austria, for the supply of fine wines is too small to be exported to any extent. As in Switzerland by far the best wines are white and in style somewhat resemble those of Yugoslavia and Hungary, since the grape varieties, usually stated on the label, include Riesling, Sylvaner, and Gewürztraminer, as well as local varieties, Rotgipfler, Veltliner, and Gumpolds-kirchner. This last, produced chiefly south of Vienna, is possibly the best known of all the Austrian wines. Though it can never be called a great wine, it has a fragrant bouquet and a light, fruity flavour, the sort of wine to drink through a summer evening, to the accompaniment of a café orchestra playing the "Blue Danube".

SWITZERLAND

The wine production of Switzerland is comparatively small,

and by far the greater number of vineyards grow white grapes. They are chiefly near the French border, and follow the course of the river Rhône, along the north shore of the lake of Geneva, where they are planted on steeply terraced hillsides.

The principal grape is the Fendant, producing light, soft, dry and very refreshing wines, excellent with fresh-water fish and the cheese dishes for which Switzerland is so famous. The main areas are the Valais, the Vaud, and Neuchatel. The wines are usually sold under their area names, but occasionally one comes across a bottle sold under the label of a *clos* or a village.

Wine is also grown around the lake at Zürich. The vines are planted on the hillsides overlooking the city and the water, whose sparkling reflection of the sun no doubt helps to radiate additional light and warmth to the vines. Yet these wines cannot compete with those of French Switzerland for character or quality. Nor can those of Ticcino, the area bordering on Italy, where experiments have been made with the Merlot grape, which, though it produces a fruity vine, cannot in any way be compared with its Bordeaux namesake.

If Switzerland does not produce any great wines, she does make a number of fresh, crisp, attractive wines which are reasonably priced and make pleasant drinking.

GREECE

Wine in ancient Greece was considered a sign of civilization, and the first act of the early Greek colonists was to plant vines wherever they settled.

Greece can certainly lay claim to being the source of the world's viticulture. It was the Greeks who evolved the method of growing vines, and they were the first to observe the paradox that the poorest soil invariably produced the finest wines. It is consequently very difficult to accept the art of which the Greeks were so proud, when faced with its interpretation in the shape of the resinated wine sold in the country today. At least half of Greece's wine production is treated with this harsh and bitter additive, since it has the property of conserving the wine against the extreme heat of the country's climate. There are, nevertheless, a number of wines which are not so treated, though this is not to say they attain any particular excellence. The unfavourable climate produces heavy, full-bodied wines, too rich in alcohol to give any delicacy or finesse. However, Greece retrieves some of her reputation with her dessert wines. The best known is without doubt the Sweet Muscat of Samos, a white wine with an alcohol content of 18 per cent.

Such wines can only be at their best when complementing the very sweet cakes and pastries, compounded of exotic ingredients such as honey, almonds, rose-water and cinnamon, which are served with dried figs and raisins.

The drier wines should partner strongly herb- and spice-flavoured dishes, the fish plakis in which the fish are baked with lemon juice, garlic, tomatoes and olive oil, the kebabs of meat threaded on to skewers, liberally seasoned with mountain herbs and grilled over a wood fire, and the highly seasoned ragouts stewed so slowly that the ingredients are reduced almost to the consistency of sauce.

CYPRUS

Wine-making has flourished in Cyprus since the time of the ancient Greeks, and as one might expect from a country bathed in sunshine for most of the year, the local taste is for full, deep-coloured, strongly-flavoured wines with a high alcohol content.

The oldest known wine is a rich dessert wine, named Commandaria by the Knights Templar to whom Richard Coeur de Lion had given the island in 1191.

The white wines, though full, tend to be dry.

Cyprus has latterly been making and exporting sherry-type wines, whose main merit is their inexpensiveness.

YUGOSLAVIA, DALMATIA AND HUNGARY

With the exception of the tourist centres on the Adriatic coast, most of the wines made in the interior are unknown in the West.

The Riesling grape is grown largely in Yugoslavia and accounts for most of the wine exported. The most famous vineyards are planted around the town of Ljutomer. While up to the present comparatively few wines have found their way to the West, a number of growers are beginning to export direct to wine merchants. The industry is growing, and though the wines can never claim the subtleties of German or French Riesling wines, they are made with care, and offer very pleasant drinking at reasonable cost. The red wines are mostly full-flavoured and inclined to be sweet. The best known is Dinjac, which is a pleasing foil to the herb-seasoned and spiced food. Yugoslavian food has many similarities with that of the Near East. The climate is not unlike and the majority of the population are farmers.

Meat is often threaded on to skewers, alternated with onions and tomatoes, seasoned liberally with mountain herbs and lemon juice, and grilled over a wood fire. They also make a version of Moussaka, a sort of ragout of minced mutton, aubergines, onions, tomatoes, garlic, and herbs stewed in olive oil. The enjoyment of these aromatic dishes is still more improved when washed down with the full local wines.

There is, however, one exception to these pleasant but undistinguished table wines—the historical Hungarian Tokay, at one time said to be the most expensive wine in the world.

As Hungary is now part of the Soviet Union, her wines are

not often found in the west of Europe. But to drink Tokay is an unforgettable experience. The greatest Tokays are sweet, with a heady flower-scented bouquet and a superb flavour. They have something of the unctuous texture of the finest Sauternes, or the Trockenbeerenauslese of the Rheingau, in their golden depths, which is not astonishing, since the syrup extract, known as Eszencia, is made largely of *botrytis* grapes.

Other white wines of quality are made from the Riesling grape, and also the Furmint, the grape used in Tokay. All these wines have a lusciousness and a deeply perfumed bouquet recalling earthy fertility and southern sun.

Bull's Blood, as its name implies, is a powerful red wine, and the one most frequently exported. Dark in colour, it has at its best an unexpected warmth and suppleness.

U.S.S.R.

I think it would be fair to say that the French are the most individualistic people in the world—at any rate as far as the domestic arts are concerned, which is probably one of the reasons why they produce a greater variety of wines and foods than any other nation.

If you put a pencil on the spot marking Bordeaux and draw a horizontal line to the east you will eventually arrive at the peninsula of the Crimea, the most prolific wine-producing area of the Soviet Union. But there is little resemblance between French and Soviet wines, the production of the latter being mainly a standardized one. The most distinguished wine is a dessert one made from the Muscat grape, which, conforming to the national taste for sweet wines, has a heavy bouquet and an almost syrupy texture.

Of the table wines the best are the reds, and of those I have tasted the most characteristic are those of Moldavia (formerly a province of Rumania). These are pleasantly scented, and given a background of somewhat pungent food, can make interesting drinking.

The white wines are made chiefly in Georgia, and vary from light and dry to full and sweet. The dry have an aromatic finish, which I find provides a most palatable foil for the more oily types of fish. According to leaflets advertising the wines of the Soviet Union, new areas of vines are being planted yearly, but I doubt if one can expect an improvement of the present standard, which, if not very unique, is, as far as my rather limited experience goes, consistent and sound.

NORTH AFRICA

It seems strange that along the fertile strip of land running parallel with the north coast of the Mediterranean, consumption of the wine produced from the prolific vineyards should be enjoyed only outside these territories. But Moslems are forbidden by their faith from drinking any kind of alcoholic beverage.

Wine was made and exported to Rome in the days of the classical Emperors. Although both the fresh and dried grapes continued to be cultivated, production of wine lapsed until the middle of the last century, when French colonists settling in Algeria, Morocco and Tunis, introduced their viticultural skills and founded the flourishing industry which exists today.

The majority of the wines are red and tend to be heavy in flavour and dark purple in colour, as one would expect from grapes ripened under a tropically hot sun.

Until recently the wines of Algeria were sold mainly for blending with feeble—i.e., weak in alcoholic strength—French wines of poor years. Now Algerian wines, particularly those from the mountainous regions, have developed a character of their own, fruity and supple, often with a certain quality. They should be drunk young.

SOUTH AFRICA

South Africa has a three-hundred-year-tradition of wine making. The important vineyards lie at the south-westerly tip of the country. Although most of the vine varieties were originally imported from Europe, many of the wines have developed quite individual characteristics. Indeed a grape called Steen is certainly a successor of the vines planted by the early settlers of the seventeenth century. The wines made from this grape are of Riesling type, and generally have a fine dry character, with an agreeable lightness and fragrance.

The best sweet white wines come from Constantia, an area with an unbroken record since 1679 for high-quality dessert wines.

The majority of red wines are strong and dark, and favour the full-bodied style of the Rhône. The principal areas where they are grown are Constantia, Stellenbosch and Paarl, the first two districts being near the coast. (Proximity to water is always advantageous to vine production.)

It is really in the making of dessert wines—port and sherry types—that South Africa has built up her reputation. The climate greatly resembles that of the Iberian peninsula, and the skill with which the grapes are treated ensures excellent quality.

Holland has been the main buyer of the South African brandy, sold under the name of Van der Hum. It was first made in the seventeenth century and was chiefly distinguished for its flavour of tangerines. Touched with rum, it is a most comforting liquor to drink at the end of a winter supper. It is said to owe its name to the Dutch settlers, who unable to remember the name of the proprietor called it Van der Hum (What's-his-name).

All South African brandies are distilled and matured under strict government supervision, and though they cannot be compared to the silky cognacs of France, when certified by the Government Brandy Board to be distilled from pure wine brandy, they make a most welcome addition to a cellar.

AUSTRALIA

The history of Australian wine begins in 1788, when Captain Arthur Phillip, the first Governor of New South Wales, planted a row of vine cuttings, which he had brought with him among a consignment of 'plants for the settlement'. From this three-acre vineyard has developed one of Australia's major industries.

Until well into the nineteenth century viticulture was the hobby of rich men, who made wine purely for their own consumption, and it was not till the interest in production had spread to the new colony of Victoria that in 1820 the first commercial vineyard was planted on the outskirts of Sydney by John Macarthur, who had made a journey through France to study wine cultivation. He returned to Australia 'stuffed with information and loaded with cuttings'. By 1827 he had increased his production to the astonishing figure of 20,000 gallons, and by the end of the 1830's a number of other growers had followed his example and had bought land in the fertile southern valleys. Numerous strains of European grapes were imported, and included Riesling, Cabernet, Shiraz (the grape of Persian origin called in Europe Syrah, and used in the vineyards of Côtes du Rhône), Tokay and Verdelho, associated with white port.

Australia makes almost every type of still wine, and also produces interpretations of sparkling wines, dessert wines and brandies.

Today wine is made in many parts of the enormous territories whose variations of soil and climate offer unlimited possibilities to the grower. The main areas are the Barossa valley (in New South Wales), chiefly devoted to the production of dessert wines. The vineyards on the higher ground are mainly used for the cultivation of Riesling-type, and dry red wines.

The Hunter valley is one of the few areas in the world where the vines are grown on their own roots. It is an old-established district known for red and white table wines of special quality.

Rutherglen, developed in the early days of the new colonies, enjoys long hot summers, resulting in sweet dessert wines, particularly port and sherry types. These regions are not irrigated, and depend for their moisture on the annual rainfall, which can attain 20 inches or more in good years.

The vineyards of the irrigated areas are mostly run as co-operatives, producing dried fruit as well as large outputs of brandy. The export of wine is controlled by the Australian Wine Board and it seems unfortunate that the finest wines of Australia never leave the country, for those which are exported are unable to compare with their European counterparts.

U.S.A.

The Western world has unfortunately had little opportunity to sample the finest wines of the United States, those of California, for the output of the vineyards to the north and south of San Francisco is not large enough even to supply the demands of the Union. In this area a few vineyards, whose vines were imported from France, produce superb wines which compare in quality and character with the French wines, whose style has been splendidly emulated.

It must be remembered that America's whole liquor trade suffered during the years 1920–33, when prohibition forbade 'the manufacture, sale, or transportation of intoxicating liquors within the importation thereof into, or the exportation thereof from the United States and all territory subject to the

jurisdiction thereof for beverages purposes is hereby pro-
hibited'. The result can be imagined. The immediate formations
of systems for illicit sales of products sold under innocuous
labels, the smuggling into the country of any kind of spirit from
Europe, the 'speak-easies' where it might be consumed, and the
'bootleggers' who marketed the stuff. Strange beers were
brewed in home cellars, gin was camouflaged under medicinal
labels, but wines were legally allowed to be made and sold for
sacramental purposes.

During the thirteen and a half years of this dismal experi-
ment producers tended their vines and made wine, so that
when the Amendment was repealed and States were allowed to
choose for themselves whether they would remain 'dry', or
vote 'wet', California was one of the first to pick up the
traditions of wine-making introduced by Cortez in the sixteenth century.

Many of the vines planted at the beginning of the present
century were imported by European immigrants expecting to
make fortunes from the fabled Klondyke. It follows that these
vines were of the *vitis vinifera* species, and include the more
familiar varieties from France, Germany and Italy. The wines
made from these grapes follow pretty faithfully their European
counterparts. Sparkling wines and dessert wines are also made,
but there is no doubt that the red and white table wines from
the Napa valley and Sonoma take the lead in distinction. There
is one grape, indigenous to the area, which makes agreeable
light red wines, something after the style of Beaujolais, called
the Zinfandel.

Wine is also made in the eastern States, largely from
American grapes which cannot be compared with the species
vitis vinifera. Although they are often blended with European
grape varieties, the juice from American vines always contains
a characteristic 'foxiness' Europeans need to become accustomed to. Wines made from the best known of these, a dark
blue grape called Concord, are widely planted in New York

State and the surrounding country. They are chiefly used for making sweet sparkling wines and Kosher wines.

CANADA

Up to the time of writing Canadian wines may be sold only to the Liquor Control Boards by the wineries producing them. They are consequently unknown outside their country. Grapes are grown principally in the Niagara peninsula, and in British Columbia. So far most of the wines are of sweet dessert type, but production of table varieties is increasing.

ARGENTINA

Although during the last forty years or so the methods of wine production in the Argentine have been steadily improving, it is only very recently that the countries of the West have had the opportunity to taste the results. In spite of her enormous production, the Argentinian is a far from niggardly drinker and up to the last few years has consumed every drop he has produced. Now Argentina contests with Spain for the third place in quantity of production.

Grapes have been grown, and wine made in Argentina since the sixteenth century. But it was not until three hundred years later that Italian immigrants brought both the vines and methods of production from Europe.

The best wines are made from classic European vines, including Riesling, Pinot-Chardonnay, Sauvignon, Cabernet and Malbec. The white wines are more dry and refreshing than one would expect from such a hot country, but I was particularly impressed by two claret-type wines made from the Cabernet grape, the one made by the firm of Orfila, the other, which I found especially successful, made by the firm of Toso (and sold as Cabernet Toso) who also produce an agreeable *rosé*. All these wines are non-vintage. At the time of writing they cost under £1 and are, I think, quite excellent value.

CHILE

Within the last fifty years the reputation of Chilean wines has grown to the extent that she is now rated thirteenth among the wine-producing countries. Vines were introduced in the sixteenth century by the Spaniards, but it was not until 1851 that the industry received its first real impetus, when Silvestre Ochagavia brought in a number of French viticultural experts with, at the same time, cuttings from vines considered suitable for the Chilean soil and climate. How fortunate was his decision can be judged from the quality of most of the wines, which today are exported to many countries.

The most important vineyards are those planted in the central section of the country. The majority of the wines are red, of Bordeaux character and type, and are of a quite outstanding quality. But there are also some excellent white wines, both of Riesling and Bordeaux and dry Loire style.

To the south the soil is not so well adapted, and though some satisfactory wines are made, they have neither the breed nor the finesse of their neighbours. From the north of the country come fortified wines.

Chilean wines are classified into four categories, *Courant* for wines one year old, *Special* between two and four years, *Reserve* from four to six years, and *Gran Vino* applies to wines over six years old. They are all excellent value for money.

There are, of course, many other wine-producing countries but I have only included wines from those countries that I have been able to assess personally and from countries that up to the time of writing export their wines in any appreciable quantity.

THREE

Sparkling Wines

🦎

The best-known of all sparkling wines is, of course, Champagne. Although a number of countries besides France make sparkling wines on the same principle, and often name them Champagne, only those made from grapes grown within the comparatively small area around Reims have the right to the appellation Champagne.

In all good quality sparkling wines the sparkle is a purely natural development, even though it is introduced into the wine by man's hand. You could compare the process with the formation of a cultured pearl in an oyster. Man introduces into the bivalve an irritant, causing the oyster to secrete a substance which ultimately becomes a pearl.

In sparkling wines a secondary fermentation is induced by the introduction into the wine of additional sugar and yeasts (already component parts of all wines). In Champagne this second fermentation takes place after the wine is bottled. During the following nine to twelve months the bottles are racked in wooden frames like double-sided boards, except that holes are cut in rows just large enough to hold the neck of the bottle. The bottles are stored neck downwards, in order that the cellarman can give each bottle a good shake every few days, not only to aromatize the added mixture with the wine, but to drive the sediment down towards the cork. By the time all the deposit has accumulated in the neck of the bottle, the carbonic acid gas (which in a still wine has been allowed to escape) has built up to a pressure five or six times that of the atmosphere outside. (This is why a sparkling wine bottle is always made of much thicker glass than an ordinary wine bottle and why the cork is held by a strong wire cage.)

The wine is now ready to undergo the process which will eject the sediment. This is done by freezing the neck of the bottle and removing the cork. The force of the pressure shoots out the sediment, now frozen into a tube-shaped plug of ice. The amount of wine lost is replaced by a *liqueur de tirage*, wine mixed with a little sugar (the amount depends on how sweet a wine the shipper intends to make), and often a drop or two of brandy as a final stabilizer. The wine is now corked and the cork clamped by a wire to keep it in position.

Besides Champagne, the adjacent vineyards of the Loire produce delicious sparkling wines. The most famous are Saumur and Vouvray, both of which tend to be sweeter than Champagne, and the grape flavour more pronounced.

German sparkling wines are called *Sekt*. Although most of them are made by the Champagne method, a number of shippers have turned to a modern interpretation of this old tradition. Instead of fermenting the wines in individual bottles, they are developed in glass-lined tanks, one could almost say in an enormous bottle. After the natural yeasts have converted the grape sugar into alcohol and other substances, the wines are filtered and left for a year to stabilize and mature. The blending of the wines then takes place, and they are transferred to new tanks (also glass-lined). The sugar and yeasts are now added, and an electric mixer aromatizes the wine with all the valuable ingredients in the yeast. This process takes about a month instead of, as formerly, a year. But . . . a reputable firm does not bottle the wines till they have been allowed to rest for a further six months, when the wine is again filtered.

German sparkling wines are less alcoholic than Champagne. While a producer may buy wines from other countries, the reputable firms use principally German wines.

Italy is famous for a sparkling wine called Asti Spumante— sweet, and given the right conditions, refreshing. Both Spain and Portugal make sparkling wines, generally by the *Méthode Champénoise*, as described at the beginning of this chapter. In the United States sparkling wines are made in most wine-producing areas, the best coming from California and the regions of New York State. The wines tend to be sweet.

Sparkling wines are also made by the principal shippers in Australia, by both the *Méthode Champénoise* and fermentation in tank. They are not as a rule exported.

The beauty of all sparkling wines made by the above two methods lies in the vertical columns of infinitesimal bubbles which ascend to form a *creamy* (not frothy) lid at the top of the glass. The better the quality of production the smaller the bubbles will be.

There is also a method of making sparkling wine by pumping carbonic acid gas into the wine. But this is only used for the very cheapest wines, and the wine never properly foams. It bubbles when poured out, and then goes flat.

Sparkling wines are an ideal aperitif, but they can also be drunk very enjoyably throughout a meal. They go particularly well with cold food—fish, poultry, galantines, salads, cheeses and summer fruits.

FOUR

Fortified Wines

Almost until the beginning of the Second World War, no dinner party was considered complete unless sherry was served with the soup, and port with the cigars. Nowadays port is sometimes served as an apéritif, and sherry with dessert.

Both these wines, and the half-dozen or so others within the range are known as fortified wines. That is to say, their natural alcohol content is increased by the addition of spirit (usually grape brandy) to approximately double that of table wines. The majority of these wines are produced in the southern part of Europe—Spain, Portugal, Sicily and Madeira.

With the exception of the Fino sherries, the general character of the wines is rich, full and unmistakably 'grapey' on the palate. They are to be sipped rather than drunk.

Although the grapes are grown in individual vineyards nearly all the wines are blended.

SHERRY

Wine was made in Jerez de la Frontera by the Phoenicians over a thousand years before the Romans occupied the town, which takes its name from the Moorish Seris, and the Latin Xeres. Shakespeare was an admirer of sherries, as is clear from his plays. The vineyards are planted around the town which lies a few miles from the coast, midway between Gibraltar and the Portuguese frontier. The climate is hot, and the grapes grow in chalky soil, baked under the scorching sun to bone whiteness. The only colour in this arid Andalusian landscape is given by the vines.

There are two features in the production of sherry which make it different from other fortified wines. They are the appearance of *flor*, and blending by the *solera* system. *Flor* is a yeast which forms a greyish white scum on the surface of the wine. It settles after the wine has been fermenting for about three months, and as the casks are not sealed (as they are in the case of most wines) the *flor* grows. It does not develop on all wines— only on the *Finos* whose alcohol level is low enough to support it.

The grapes are gathered in late September and are laid in the sun in order that some of the juice shall evaporate. They are then pressed, and fermentation begins, violently at first, slowing down after a week or ten days, till all the sugar has been converted into alcohol. At the end of about three months fermentation is usually complete, and the wines are classified into two types: *Finos*, on which *flor* has developed, and *Rayas*, which are eventually fortified more strongly, and which develop into a sweeter style of sherry called *Oloroso*. The wines are tasted regularly during this period, for, by one of those inexplicable mysteries connected with wine, a *Fino* may, during the course of its evolution, change its character for apparently no reason, and take on the nature of a *Raya*.

It is only when the producer is perfectly satisfied that the wines will develop no further that they are taken to the *bodegas* and transferred to the blending casks.

The *solera* system, complicated though it may appear, is based on the straightforward principle of passing on the characteristics of the oldest wines to the youngest. This is done by placing the newest wines in the *criadera* (cradle) butts, which already contain young sherries. In a four-tier *solera*, for example, the first butt contains the young wines, and the fourth (the *solera*) the finished mature wine. When a shipper intends to bottle he draws off a quantity of the oldest wine from the *solera*, and fills up the space with younger wine from the first *criadera*. The space in the first *criadera* is topped up with still younger wine from the second *criadera*, which in its turn is replaced with new wines.

It is important that the young wines be similar in style and quality to the wine in which they are introduced, for only in this way they will be absorbed into the character of the mature wine. It is this measure which gives his sherries the shipper's 'hall-mark'.

Sherries are developed as we have said into two types—*Finos*, of dry character, *Rayas*, heavier and sweeter. The driest of all *finos* is Manzanilla, which is produced at Sanlucar de Barrameda, an area on the coast. These wines are so dry as to leave an almost salty taste on the tongue. Indeed, it is said that the briny atmosphere is responsible. At any rate they have a crispness and elegance which make them almost unparalleled as the perfect apéritif. Slightly chilled and sipped with nibblings of olives or salted almonds, they should whip up even the most blasé appetite.

Amontillado, while still of a dry character, has a definite nuttyness which gives a more pungent taste. It is darker in colour than a *fino*, from which it develops, and paler than an *Oloroso*. The *Olorosos* are all more suitable as dessert wines. They are sweeter, more full bodied, and deep golden in colour. The cream sherries are usually fine old *Olorosos*, golden-brown in colour, and have the typical intense *Oloroso* sweetness. Brown sherries, developed from *Rayas*, almost approach Madeiras in their richness and depth of colour and flavour.

PORT

Gone are the days of the 'three-bottle' drinkers of port, and gone, regrettably, are the owners of cellars who, as a matter of course, laid down pipes of vintage port. (A pipe is a cask holding 115–17 gallons). Nowadays port is drunk as often before a meal as a satisfying termination to one. It can be drunk chilled; it can be drunk at room temperature. Yet with all this versatility its production is controlled by more restrictions than any other wine. To begin with, its name may only be used for wines of the Upper Douro, which are fortified by Portuguese grape brandy and shipped from Oporto, the town which has given port its name.

Like Bordeaux, Oporto faces the Atlantic, and until recently more port was shipped to England than to any other country. Like Bordeaux, Portugal traded extensively with Great Britain in the eighteenth century and, reasonably enough, a number of Englishmen established themselves in the area of Oporto as shippers. The most famous names in the port trade are English and Scottish ones—Croft, Taylor, Cockburn, Warre, Dow, Sandeman, Graham, Mackenzie, Delaforce—and the wines were primarily intended for the British taste.

The *quintas*, or vineyards, are planted along terraces cut in the very steep cliffs bordering the river. The climate is one of extremes, tropically hot in the summer, with no rain to lay the dust which is continually blown by the west winds, and bitterly cold in the winter.

The process of making port differs from other fortified wines in that, in order to achieve the luscious richness characteristic of most ports, fermentation is checked at an early stage by the addition of large doses of brandy. Fermentation starts immediately the grapes have been pressed. After a few days the juice is fortified with grape brandy and run off into vats called pipes, and the wine is 'roused' (by rolling the casks) to ensure that it is thoroughly blended with the brandy. It is now stored, and remains through the winter in the *quinta*. In the spring, when the impurities and dead yeast cells have sunk to the bottom of the cask, the wine is transferred to clean casks and taken to the wine lodges to mature for a further year, when it will have developed its own character and quality. During this period it will be blended with other wines from the same vintage.

According to Portuguese law, the wines must remain in the lodges for a specified period, during which they are classified and blended, so that a consistent quality for the different types is maintained.

With the exception of vintage port, all port is aged in casks, and bottled only when the shipper has satisfied himself it is ready to drink. Nearly all port is bottled in the country where it will be drunk, so it is absolutely essential to buy a recognized and reputable brand. The ports which undergo this treatment are called Ruby and Tawny. Ruby, the youngest, is fresh and fruity, and should be drunk soon after it is bottled. If the wines are left for ten or fifteen years in the casks the bright redness will have faded and taken on something of the colour of the cask. Tawny port develops an exquisite bouquet and a delicious nutty flavour. The sign of a true old tawny wine is the brown 'bead' that becomes apparent when the glass is held against a light background. 'Bead' is the thinnest point of colour in the wine as seen against the side of the glass. Of all the categories of port, tawny is the most versatile.

In really outstanding years the shippers set the best wines aside in order to make vintage port. The wines selected for vintage port are shipped two years or so after their vintage, mostly to London, where they are bottled at once. While the other ports age in casks, vintage ports are always laid down in glass. They are of necessity a long-term investment, since they need between ten and twenty years to achieve maturity. Their peak, however, is reached still later, for they continue to improve for a long time. The longer port is kept, the more 'crust' (a thick sediment) it will throw. The bottles should be stored with the labels uppermost, so that the crust will collect on the side opposite the label. Before being used the bottle should be allowed to stand for forty-eight hours, when the wine should be carefully decanted through fine muslin, making sure, as you pour, that the label remains uppermost.

Although the valley of the Douro is essentially red wine country, a small amount of white grapes are grown and used to make a dry wine which is fortified, and intended to be drunk chilled before a meal. Though it makes a pleasant change, it lacks the vitality of an equivalent sherry.

MADEIRA

When the extinct volcanic island of Madeira first appeared before the eyes of Captain Zarco, sent to claim it for Portugal in 1418, it consisted of a forest so thick that it was impossible to penetrate. Zarco named it Madeira (the wood) and, finding no other means to conquer its dense vegetation, set it on fire. The fire raged, it is said, without interruption for seven years. When it had finally burned itself out, the trees had been transformed into a soil of unbelievable fertility. It is in this soil that the colonists planted the vines on the perpendicular slopes of the island, accessible only to man and donkey.

The production of Madeira differs from other fortified wines in that as soon as fermentation is complete, the wines are fortified and stored, in heated rooms called *estufas*, at a high temperature for a minimum of six months. (The word *estoufat*, or *estouffade*, often occurs in French and Italian cookery and means the slow cooking of meat or vegetables in a hermetically sealed pan or cocotte. Such dishes are also described as *à l'étuvée*—steamed.)

This method of maturation gives the wines their very individual caramelized, and sometimes smoky, taste.

Madeira is the most long-living wine in the world. The celebrated shipper, John Blandy, bottled in 1842 a Madeira which was reputed to be 141 years old. It had been bought for Napoleon in exile and had not been touched.

There are four main varieties of grapes grown, and the wines are called after them. Each produces a totally different type of wine.

Sercial is the driest of the four, and is considerably lighter in colour than the others. It makes an excellent apéritif.

Verdelho is less dry than *Sercial*, and more golden in colour. It has a smooth quality, which makes it agreeable before or after a meal.

Bual is a typical dessert wine, golden brown in colour, and with a particularly velvety depth.

Malmsey (named after the Malvasia grape) is the richest and darkest. It matures to a great age, and is the fullest and sweetest in flavour.

MALAGA

Malaga is a Spanish dessert wine with a pronounced flavour of raisins. The wines tend to be big, sweet and long-living.

MARSALA

Marsala, whose alcoholic strength matches both port and sherry, has great affinities with sherry. It is made in Sicily from white grapes growing in volcanic soil, and is generally fortified as a sweet dessert wine, though the type called Virgin has a marked degree of dryness, and a nutty, deep flavour.

FIVE

Distilled Wines

🦁

Any spirit which has been distilled from wine becomes brandy. The first brandy is said to have come into existence by one of those fortunate chances, when a Dutch sea captain of the sixteenth century, trying to save space in his ship, concentrated a shipment of wine from Cognac by boiling it down and by the end of the voyage had, one imagines to his surprise, produced brandy. This fluke led to regular practice of the operation, the idea being to lessen the volume of the wines by reducing them and reconstituting them with water when required.

COGNAC

All distilled wines are brandies. Cognac, the most famous of all brandies, is the name of a place in France where the finest of all grape brandies is made. No other area in the world is allowed to use the name Cognac on a label. Like Champagne, brandy is blended and its production can take anything up to twenty years. The wines are distilled by heating them in massive copper kettles called pot stills. The still is sealed and the wine is brought to the boil, when all the volatile substances, including the alcohol, are distilled into vapour which is then condensed and collected in a tank. This liquid, called the 'heart' of the brandy, after a second distillation is by now reduced to a colourless spirit. Once distilled the spirit is transferred to oak barrels, where it is matured for anything between three and fifty years. At this point two very important factors come into play. The quality of the oak is paramount, for if too young a wood is used it can not only spoil the taste of the brandy, but can also darken the spirit too deeply while it is developing.

The atmosphere of the cellar, too, is crucial. During the twenty or more years that the average brandy must remain in the cask the alcohol gradually evaporates. The drier the cellar the greater the evaporation. This evaporation would in forty or fifty years reduce a brandy of 70 per cent alcoholic strength (far too harsh and fiery to drink) to about half. As such a long natural wait is obviously quite impracticable, the strength of brandies is reduced by diluting them gradually with distilled water. The *département* of the Charente embraces quiet arable and dairy country . . . and Cognac, whose vineyards cover an area of about 250 square miles. The grapes which account for the finest brandy in the world produce undistinguished, almost tart wines. The best areas are around the town of Cognac, and are called Grande Champagne and Petite Champagne. They are responsible for at least 20 per cent of all cognacs. They are either sold under their individual names or blended together and sold as Fine Champagne, on condition that at least 50 per cent Grande Champagne is used in the blend.

The next area is called Les Borderies, and while not reaching the same delicacy and finesse of Fine Champagne, a very respectable brandy is made. Beyond this area come Fins Bois and Bons Bois, making a much more common spirit. The border of the whole district is called Bois Ordinaires and Bois Communs. These areas are responsible for all the types of cognac sold. About 90 per cent is marketed under the heading of Three Star. This does not mean that the brandy is three years old. It is an indication that the quality is better than a bottle labelled merely Cognac. V.S.O.P. (standing for Very Superior Old Pale) means that the wine may have twenty or more years of barrel age. You may also see bottles labelled Reserve, Extra or Cordon Bleu.

I feel I should here mention those cobwebbed bottles labelled 'Napoleon', and at the risk of disillusioning romantic readers, state categorically that any brandy kept in barrel since his life-time would long since have evaporated, and any that had been kept in bottle would have certainly deteriorated, since brandy once bottled ceases to improve.

ARMAGNAC AND EAUX-DE-VIE

Armagnac. Few people are familiar with the delights of Armagnac, a brandy made from white grapes grown in Gascony, lying between Bordeaux and the Spanish frontier, an area of oak and pine forests on the one hand, and streams breaking up the monotony of the spreading plains on the other. Most Armagnacs have great finesse and an aroma so individual that they can never be confused with any other type of brandy.

Grape brandies are made in other countries besides France. The best of them come from Spain and South Africa.

There is also a spirit distilled from pulped grapes or other fruits after the juice has been run off. It is called Marc. The best-known Marcs come from Burgundy and Champagne, but Alsace also makes excellent ones from cherries and plums.

Eaux-de-vie. A number of brandies are distilled from fruits other than grapes. They differ from other brandies in that they are neither sweetened nor coloured. Most of the varieties are made in Alsace, where almost as much fruit grows as vines.

The main varieties are Kirsch, distilled from the black cherries which border nearly all the Alsatian roads, Framboise, perhaps the rarest, made from raspberries gathered in the Vosges—their delicate, almost elusive, fragrance the very essence of the fruit, Quetsch, a blue plum spirit, native of both Alsace and Lorraine, Mirabelle, rather similar to Quetsch, distilled from small yellow plums grown around Nancy and Metz, and Slivovitz, a double distilled plum brandy from Yugoslavia and the Balkans.

There is one other fruit brandy which comes from the north-west of France. I mean, of course, Calvados, the *eau-de-vie* associated with the crisp sharp-scented apples of Normandy.

SIX

Apéritifs and Liqueurs

The object of an apéritif is to stimulate the appetite. The object of a liqueur is to settle it. Apéritifs are therefore mostly dry and liqueurs sweet. Apéritifs combine excellently with salted nuts, olives, certain salty fish and cheese. Since a liqueur should slake the appetite it should, I suppose, by rights be drunk after all the food is eaten. Yet liqueurs, I think, are improved when balanced against a sweet biscuit such as macaroons or petit fours.

The best preparations for a meal are dry champagne, dry German sparkling wine, pale dry sherry, any dry white wine, vermouth and the brand apéritifs made on a vermouth base and flavoured with herbs and spices, and a range of others flavoured with quinine or bitters. Vermouth can be red or white, sweet or dry; it is made in France and Italy, though by far the greater amount comes from Italy. The best-known French vermouths are Noilly Prat and Chambéry. The labels of Cinzano and Martini are known all over the world.

Examples of the quinine-tasting apéritifs are Punt e Mes from Italy and Quinquina from France.

Bitters provide the piquancy in Campari, Amer Picon and Suze (tinctured with gentian). These should be diluted with aerated water and served iced. Indeed, most apéritifs gain by being served chilled.

While apéritifs are of comparatively recent invention, liqueurs are a far from modern idea. Roots and herbs were grown by the monks of the Middle Ages for their medicinal properties, and in the thirteenth century a Catalan physician is known to have written a treatise on the properties of herbs extracted by alcohol. Wines mixed with herbs and particles of gold, besides such exotic ingredients as amber, cinnamon and musk, were considered a panacea for many ills. Rum was a valuable addition when it began to be imported from the newly-established colonies in the Pacific.

The usual method of making these liqueurs was to macerate the fruits and flowers, and to distil a spirit from the roots, seeds and fruit kernels. Sweetening was added to make a syrupy solution. Aniseed (or caraway) is a spice much used in the east of Europe. (One of the less pleasant habits of Baroness Lehzen, Queen Victoria's governess, was said to have been her constant chewing of caraway seeds.) France, Russia, Poland and the Baltic countries all make versions of an aniseed-flavoured liqueur, though Holland and Germany claim to have been the inventors. The best known aniseed liqueurs are Anisette Marie Brizard, made in Bordeaux from a West Indian formula, and a number sold under the brand name of Kümmel.

Oranges are a favourite flavouring for liqueurs. The earliest was made from the skins of oranges growing on the Dutch-owned island of Curaçao. It became so popular that many distillers found ways of producing their own versions, the most favoured being Cointreau and Grand Marnier.

Cherries form the base of several liqueurs. Yugoslavia first formulated the recipe for Maraschino, now made chiefly in Italy. Its mysterious flavour incorporates for me something, too, of the sweet bitterness of the kernel in a peach stone.

There is a small number of liqueurs whose composition has remained a secret for hundreds of years. The most famous are Benedictine, first made at the beginning of the sixteenth century in the Benedictine monastery at Fécamp, in Normandy, and Chartreuse, made to a formula given to the monks of the Carthusian order about a hundred years later. Both these liqueurs are made on a base of brandy and flavoured with extracts of plants.

SEVEN

Dining and Wining

✤

We usually talk about wine and food, though more often than not the choice of food takes precedence over the choice of wine. We cannot live without food. On the other hand, the people of many countries would consider a meal incomplete without the partnership of wine.

During the last fifty years or so, our eating habits have been radically transformed by the invention of the refrigerator. Previously meat, except that produced in country districts for local customers, could scarcely be called fresh, and dishes were highly spiced to hide the powerful natural odours. The wines accordingly tended to be served older and fuller. Today we are able to enjoy the savour of freshly-killed meat, poultry and fish, and consequently the preparation does not require the elaborate camouflage of complicated sauces. This has resulted in a trend to drink wines much younger than formerly.

Fresh food invites the charm of young wines.

The following menus are intended as a guide to give wine its proper place as an integral part of a meal, and not just a thirst-quenching appendage. The menus are of varying degrees of cost, all are seasonal, and it will be seen that to enjoy a rare and expensive wine it is not always necessary to drink it with what I call status-symbol food, which is not necessarily a sign of good taste and discrimination. Inexpensive food can be delicious if it is chosen and prepared with imagination.

It will be noticed that soup plays a minimal part in the selection of foods. As a general rule I do not advise drinking any wine with soup. In spite of the difference in consistency I always think the one liquid cancels out the other. Wine *in* soup is a totally different thing. But a glass of dry sherry can act as an appetizer when drunk with a clear consommé.

In those menus which include cheese, please note that it is served *before* the sweet course. This order is always followed in France and Italy, where the main wine, or often the only one, is more frequently red than white. It enables whatever wine remains in the bottle after accompanying the main meat course to be finished with the cheese—always an ideal complement to any red wine. My own personal preference is to serve port either with cheese or nuts. I find the slightly bitter fragrance of coffee, and maybe the fact that it is another liquid, disturbing rather than adding to my enjoyment of the luscious character of the wine. I find a glass of fine cognac a better bonus.

When planning any meal to be eaten with a good wine, be sparing with the vinegar bottle. As its name suggests, it is made from sour wine (*vin aigre*). One part to five parts of oil is enough to season a salad. Avoid raw oranges or grapefruit. I am also not enthusiastic over bananas, either raw or cooked, with any kind of wine. Tomatoes, peppers or aubergines are not always happy when combined with any kind of white wines. Being natives of the south, they unite much more successfully with the red wines of the Mediterranean countries.

Never serve chocolate sweets, or sweets with a chocolate sauce, with any wine. The one will kill the other. Sweets buried under mounds of whipped cream should also be avoided. But any sauce in which cream is an ingredient, and therefore cooked, will enrich the dish it accompanies.

Any dish marinated in wine should be served with the same type of wine. For example, meat marinated and stewed in Burgundy (you can buy a cheap one for this) should be eaten with a wine from that region.

Red wine, particularly red Bordeaux, combines excellently

with cherries, pears and pippy fruits such as strawberries, raspberries, currants, gooseberries and blackberries.

The wines I have chosen for each menu are intended to be suggestions.

As your wine merchant may not have the particular one I have recommended, you will find at the end of this book a list of wines from the major areas, so that if you are unable to buy the one I have specified you can select a similar alternative. There are also many varieties of wines mentioned in the text.

POSTSCRIPT

The 1971 German wine laws have reduced the number of individual vineyards, the smaller ones in an area selling their wines under the umbrella of the best-known vineyards of the group.

The law has laid down three basic grades of quality, and the description must appear on all labels:

Tafelwein, which, roughly corresponding to French *vin ordinaire*, is not allowed to use a vineyard name and is not bound to make wine of any particular strength or quality, or come from any particular area or grape variety.

Qualitätswein is a table wine which has to come from a particular area, from particular grape varieties. The label also has to carry a test number, e.g., AP No. . . . followed by letters and figures.

Qualitätswein mit Prädikat. This description applies only to first quality wines, whose production is strictly controlled. They must be made only from certain varieties of grape, come from particular areas, they may not be sugared, and their *must* (the unfermented juice from the newly-pressed grapes) must attain a certain weight. This last grade must also state the category of natural sweetness—*Kabinett, Spätlese, Auslese, Beerenauslese, Trockenbeerenauslese, Eiswein*—on the label. The label in addition should bear a description: *Aus Eigener Abfüllung* (bottled by the producer) followed by the name. It must also carry a test number.

Similar laws apply to the production of sparkling wines. The lowest category will be described as *Schaumwein* (sparkling wine). A better quality will be labelled *Sekt*. The top quality sparkling wines must bear the description *Prädikat*, indicating that at least 60 per cent German wine has been used in the production, and that they must be stored for a minimum of nine months under pressure.

As with the top-quality still wines, *Sekt* in the higher categories must also bear an official test number.

II

Food

EIGHT

Cheese

🦎

It is a curious fact that while one of the happiest marriages between wine and food is the one between wine and cheese, there is not, so far as I know, any area in the world where good cheese-producing regions produce high-quality wine, or where great wine-producing regions produce first-quality cheeses. Consequently the most harmonious combinations of cheese and wine are the result of proved experiments since man first discovered the delectable combination.

Cheese, like wine, develops by ripening—often, like wine, over a period of years. Like wine, too, it is made of a single product, milk, which contains some of the same elements as wine—yeasts and acids, for example.

As wine producers in the New World have imported vines from Europe, so cheese makers have adopted methods of producing cheeses often several thousands of miles away from the original area. While there must, of course, be resemblances, even with the greatest attention the results—however appetizing —cannot but be copies. Imported grape varieties may, and often do, produce delightful wines (Californian Rieslings, for instance), but they have developed their own characteristics. The climate, the soil, and the type of grape determine the character and style of wine. So with cheese the breed of cow, the pasturage which provides its food, the water it drinks, result in over twelve hundred varieties in the world.

The process which converts milk into cheese is the separation of the solid of the milk from the liquid. This separation is achieved either by the addition of lactic acid, or by rennet. Both these methods curdle the milk. The first produces cheeses of the cottage or 'fresh' type. The second results in a cheese which can be ripened. The milk which forms the basis of nearly all cheeses can be from either a cow, a ewe, or a goat. The choice of milk determines the category of cheese. By far the greatest number of cheeses are made from cows' milk. The more liquid expelled from the curd, the harder the cheese will be.

There are three primary types of cheese.

The Hard-Pressed Cheeses, to which Cheddar and the better-known hard cheeses belong. This category can be sub-divided into the Emmental range, a cross between hard and soft, which includes Gouda and Edam, and the Port Salut varieties, mild in flavour and texture, midway between semi-soft and soft.

Blue Cheeses, which include Stilton, Roquefort and Gorgon-zola.

Soft Paste Cheeses, as exemplified by the Camembert and Brie family.

In addition to these three types are the goat cheeses, which vary from the soft and creamy to hard, from the mildest to the sharpest flavour.

I have long been waging a war against the manufacturers who prepack their cheeses in foil. This applies particularly to those of the Camembert and Brie type, where it is as essential to smell as well as to feel the texture and to see the colour. It is no good prodding a cheese through a thick layer of foil. If it feels soft the chances are it could be over-ripe. The crust of these cheeses should be pale and the edges should merge into the top and sides. If they incline to be sharp, the cheese is probably too old and will have an ammoniated smell. The texture should be yellow and creamy.

In buying any cheese it is important to look at the condition. If it is sweating, if it is so dry it is cracked, if the rind appears blemished, do not buy it. If it smells ammoniated, stale or rancid, it has been allowed to ripen too long, or it has been kept in too warm a place. All cheeses should be kept in the cool, preferably a larder. If, however, you have to store them in a refrigerator, choose the warmest part.

Serve cheeses on a board, and do not pre-cut them into postcard-thin slices. Neither decorate them with radish rosebuds, tomato waterlilies, lemon starfish, nor strew them with cress. If you can lay your hands on some fresh strawberry, fig or vine leaves, you can place the cheeses on these. Otherwise leave them plainly on the board and let your guests help themselves. Supply plenty of crusty fresh bread, either white or brown (never, I beg you, sliced packet bread) and, if you wish, a selection of cheese biscuits and crispbreads. Be generous with the butter which must be fresh and preferably unsalted.

For wine and cheese parties don't be too ambitious. Six or seven cheeses are enough—say, two from the Cheddar family, a blue, a goat, a Camembert or Brie, a cheese from the Gruyère/Gouda range, and one of the Port Salut varieties. Allow six to eight ounces of cheese per person, and keep your wines to two, or, at the most three. A dry white (an Alsatian, or perhaps a crisp young Hock), a Burgundy or Claret, and a vigorous Italian or Spanish red wine. Choose dry rather than sweet wines, and don't serve fine estate wines. To enjoy a really great wine you need quiet and an atmosphere free from smoke and noise to appreciate its qualities.

White wines go with many cheeses, red wines go with all. In an earlier chapter of this book I have said that there is only one drink which merits the name of WINE. By the same token there is only one food which merits the name of CHEESE.

There are on the market a number of 'processed' cheeses, which, though they make agreeable sandwich fillings, are really no more than cheese-flavoured spreads and are as far removed from the genuine article as acorns are from coffee beans. Therefore, in your eating with wine, buy only cheese made by the orthodox methods.

A LIST OF BETTER-KNOWN CHEESES WITH SUGGESTED WINES

Banon   (Côtes de Provence)
A French cheese made from goats' milk. It is cured in chestnut leaves, fermented in stone jugs and sold wrapped in fresh leaves.

Bel Paese   (Orvieto)
A soft mild cheese from Italy.

Bleu d'Auvergne   (Côte Rotie, Hermitage)
A blue cheese made in the Auvergne, approximating to a cows' milk Roquefort. The flavour is rich and sharp.

Bon Bel   (Rosé d'Anjou)
A mild French cheese resembling an unmatured Edam.

Boursault   (White Graves)
A French cream cheese often made with added herbs.

Boursin   (Vouvray)
A French cream cheese made either with added herbs or with freshly crushed peppercorns.

Bresse Bleu   (Pomerol)
A French blue cheese, with a less sharp flavour than Roquefort.

Brie   (Fleurie, Pomerol, Médoc, Chinon, Nuits,
                                           Corton, Vougeot)
One of the major French cheeses. The texture is soft and creamy, and the flavour slightly salty. When over-ripe it tastes ammoniated.

Caerphilly   (Schloss Böckelheim Nahe, White Graves,
Manzanilla Sherry)
A semi-hard cheese from Wales, with a fresh white paste and a
slightly acid taste resembling buttermilk.

Camembert   (Beaune, Vougeot, Médoc)
A major French cheese. The texture, when ripe, is creamy
yellow and the flavour slightly salty.

Cantal   (Chinon, Bourgueil)
A major French cheese in character something like Cheddar. It
is made in the Auvergne, and when properly matured has a
close texture and the slightly sharp taste of an old Cheddar.

Carré de l'Est   (Volnay)
A Camembert-type of cheese with a mild, slightly salted flavour.

Chaource   (Beaujolais and Rosé wines)
A Camembert-type of cheese from the Burgundy area.

Cheddar   (Medium Sherry, St Emilion)
A major hard-pressed English cheese with a nutty, rich
flavour.

Cheshire   (Tawny Port)
An English cheese, milder and more open-textured than
Cheddar.

Chevrotin   (Moulin à Vent)
A French goat cheese, grey-green in colour on the outside. It
can be eaten fresh or matured.

Christian IX   (Alsatian Sylvaner)
A Danish cheese seasoned with caraway seeds.

Cottage Cheese (Sparkling Moselle)
A fresh curd cheese which cannot ripen.

Coulommiers (Fleurie, Volnay, Pomerol)
Somewhat similar to Brie, it has a smooth curd, is slightly less creamy and more lightly salted.

Crémet Nantais (Muscadet)
A French cream cheese from the Loire Valley, available only in the summer.

Crottin de Chavignol (Pouilly, Chablis, Sancerre, Muscadet)
A French goat cheese, rust coloured with white flakes, with a tangy flavour.

Danablue (Châteauneuf du Pape, Cream Sherry)
The famous Danish blue cheese, with a sharp flavour, and a buttery paste. It is off-white in colour, with a blue-green mould.

Danbo (Beaujolais)
A semi-hard cows' milk Danish cheese, with a nutty taste. It has a firm texture with small regular holes.

Demi-Sel (Muscadet)
A French whole-milk cheese, soft and creamy in texture.

Dolcelatte (Frecciarossa)
A creamy blue-mould cheese from Italy, with a more delicate flavour than Gorgonzola.

Double Gloucester (Pauillac, Corton, Richebourg)
A hard-pressed full-cream English cheese, with a close and crumbly texture and a slightly acid flavour.

Edam (Moselle, Franconian Wine)
A sturdy cheese of bland flavour from north Holland.

Emmental (Muscadet, Arbois)
Real Emmental is made in Switzerland, and the milk from the
Alpine slopes gives it its characteristic sweet flavour. It is a pale-
yellow hard-pressed cheese with irregular eyes. It should not
be rubbery in texture nor insipid in flavour.

Epoisse (Châteauneuf du Pape, Chambertin,
Château Mouton-Rothschild)
A French cheese with a soft paste and a reddish crust made in
the area of Burgundy. Its slightly sharp flavour makes it an
admirable foil for deeply scented red wines.

Fontainebleau (Champagne)
A French triple-cream cheese sold in pots or cartons. It is ideal
with all soft fruits.

Fourme d'Ambert (Fleurie, Hermitage)
A good-quality French blue cheese with a flavour resembling
Roquefort.

Fromage Blanc (Sparkling Saumur, Asti Spumanti)
The name given in France to a number of cottage or cream
cheeses. They sometimes are also called by a local name.

Gorgonzola (Barbaresco, Grumello)
The major blue cheese of Italy. It has a spicy salty flavour, and a
soft creamy paste veined with green mould.

Gouda (Moselle, Saar or Ruwer)
A Dutch cheese of semi-hard texture with a mild and often
insipid flavour.

Gjetost (Amontillado Sherry)
The national cheese of Norway. It is traditionally made from
the boiled whey of goats' milk and it is toast coloured, with a
sweetish flavour and a semi-hard texture.

Gruyère (Sancerre, Pouilly Fumé)
A cooked, hard, cows'-milk cheese, pale yellow and honey-
combed with eyes. Its sweet flavour resembles the Emmental.

Jarlsberg (Mâcon, Medium Sherry)
An Emmental-type of cheese from Norway, mild in flavour.

Lancashire (Medium-dry Sherry, light Tawny Port)
An English hard-pressed cheese, soft and crumbly in texture and
mellow in flavour.

Leicester (Madeira)
An English cheese something like Cheshire, but drier and
firmer. It is deeply coloured with a full flavour.

Levroux (Sancerre, Pouilly, Muscadet)
A French goat cheese with a creamy texture and a pronounced
flavour.

Livarot (Hermitage, Côte Rotie, Corton)
A French cheese made from skim cows' milk. It has a robust
flavour and is sold wrapped in leaves.

Maroilles (Beaune, Châteauneuf du Pape, Corton)
A French cows' milk cheese of the Port Salut family. It is
bland in flavour with a distinctive aroma.

Mascarpone (Barbera)
A white, soft Italian cheese with a slightly acid flavour.

Munster (Corton, Côte, Rotie, Médoc)
A French whole-milk fermented cheese, with a bright red rind.
It belongs to the mild Gouda range.

Parmesan (Barbera)
The hardest of all cheeses when fully cured. It comes from
Italy and can only be eaten as a table cheese at three months.

Pastorello (Soave)
A soft, creamy Italian cheese, mild and sweet in flavour.

Pont l'Evèque (Bourgueil, Fleurie, Pommerol, Volnay)
A French cheese farm-made from skim cows' milk. It is yellow
in colour and has a strong flavour.

Port Salut (Bourgueil)
A French semi-hard, whole-milk, pressed cheese with a
buttery mild flavour.

Provolone (Barolo)
An Italian cheese generally made from cows' milk, whose
flavour can range from sweet to sharp. The paste is creamy-
white to yellow. It may also be smoked.

Reblochon (Beaujolais)
A French cows' milk cheese, something like a Port Salut.

Ricotta Romana (Chianti)
A rich, creamy, fresh cheese, generally made from the whey of
cows' milk.

Roquefort (Châteauneuf du Pape, Chambertin, St Julien)
The famous French blue-veined cheese, made of ewes' milk. It
has a fine, rich and well-defined flavour.

Saint Nectaire   (Chinon, Fleurie, Nuits St Georges)
A French semi-hard cows' milk cheese, usually farm-made,
with a smooth paste and a bland flavour.

Saint Paulin   (Beaujolais, Bas Médoc)
Similar to Port Salut.

Samsoe   (Rheinhessen, White Graves)
The principal Danish cheese. It is something like Emmental,
with a less sweet and less pronounced flavour.

Stilton   (Tawny or old vintage Port)
The major English blue cheese. It has a flaky texture, a delicate
blue mould in a white paste, and a delicious tang in the flavour.

Tilsiter   (A Palatinate wine)
This cheese, originally made in East Prussia, is a firm light-
yellow cheese with small round eyes and a medium to sharp
flavour.

Tomme de Savoie   (Arbois, Alsatian Gewürztraminer)
A French cows' milk cheese sometimes mixed with goats'
milk. It has a firm yellow paste, and a medium, slightly salty
flavour. It is usually covered in grape seeds, which add a certain
earthiness to the flavour.

Wensleydale   (Rheingau, Beaujolais, light Port)
A white or slightly blue English cows' milk cheese. Its flavour
can range from acid when young to mellow and sweet when
matured.

NINE

Menus and Recipes

✿

A CALENDAR OF MENUS

January

1. Champignons à la bour-
      guignonne ⎱
   Entrecôte Bercy ⎰ Gevrey-
   Cheese   Chambertin
   Poirat

2. Fish pâté   Sancerre
   Filets de porc aux fines herbes   Château Beychevelle
   Cheese. Nuts   Tawny Port

February

3. Gratin d'aubergines ⎱
   Pigeonneaux en cocotte ⎰ Côtes de Bourg
   Cheese. Fruit

4. Cornets de jambon fourrés   Bourgueil
   Veau St Emilion   Château Monbousquet
   Pommes mousseline
   Gâteau de fromage blanc   Château Climens

March

5. Saucisses en pâte ⎱
   Chou rouge à l'étuvée ⎰ Alsatian Gewürz-
   Baked apples   Traminer

6. Soufflé Parmentier
   Coulis de tomates
   Coquilles St Jacques à la   } Chablis
       Côte d'Argent
   Ananas au Kirsch   Château Suduiraut

April

7. Smoked cod's roe
   Tajine aux raisins secs   } Ljutomer Riesling
   Cheese

8. Asparagus   Pouilly Fuissé
   Sauce mousseline froide
   Gigot à la provençale   Hermitage
   Sauce à la ciboulette
   Galette aux abricots   Sparkling Vouvray

May

9. Quiche Lorraine
   Canard à la normande   } Beaujolais
   Petits pois à la française
   Cheese. Fruit

10. Flan de courgettes   Bourgogne Aligoté
    Rôti de porc chasseur   Châteauneuf de Pape
    Haricots verts
    Cheese
    Gooseberry cheese

June

11. Tomates Babua
    Terrine de poulet   } Côtes de Provence
    Salad of lettuce hearts   Pradel Rosé
    Strawberry mousse

12. Concombres aux crevettes   Château Carbonnieux
    Roast chicken   Château Mouton-
    Cheese   Rothschild
    Coeurs à la crème. Strawberries   Château d'Yquem

July
13. Cassolettes aux champignons
    Homard à l'américaine   } Champagne
    Raspberry and red-currant tart

14. Gâteau d'épinards   Pommard
    Rognons de veau au vin blanc   Pouilly Fuissé
    Cheese
    Cherries

August
15. Spaghetti Napolitaine
    Jambon sous la cendre
    Sauce madère   } Barolo
    Salad
    Fresh peaches

16. Les Acrats (Beignets
       Martiniquais)
    Escalopes de veau à la rennaise   Rully
    Salad
    Cheese
    Fresh figs   Clairette de Bié

September
17. Oeufs en meurette ménagère
    Grilled lamb chops
    Braised celery   } Nuits St Georges
    Cheese
    Apples. Pears

18. Smoked trout   Moselle
  Horseradish sauce
  Roast saddle of venison Rheingau
  Potato croquettes
  Grapes. Fresh figs   Rheingau auslese

October
19. Gratin de soles   Soave
  Gnocchis romanais   Chianti
  Coulis de tomates
  Compôte d'automne

20. Moules à la crème
  Noix de veau au citron
  Endives braisées   } Meursault
  Cheese
  Crêpes Suzette

November
21. Soufflé au fromage
  Oison au chou
  Apple purée   } Rioja
  Petits suisses. Confiture

22. Omelette Médocaine   Entre Deux Mers
  Côtes de mouton au muscat Château Palmer
  Braised celery
  English Cheddar   Cream Sherry

December
23. Salade de lentilles aux chipolatas
  Roast haunch of wild boar (or
    see suggested alternatives) } Aloxe-Corton
  Potato purée or potato croquettes
  Crème de pistaches   Marsala

24. Prawns and olives   Muscadet
  Dinde à la girondine   Château Margaux
  Brussels sprouts or braised celery
  Mince pies   Madeira

RECIPES

All recipes are for four people unless otherwise stated.

MENU I

Champignons à la bourguignonne

Choose large flat mushrooms, and allow 2 or 3 per person. Cut off the stalks and put aside. Cook the caps slowly in a mixture of oil and butter. Baste the mushrooms by spooning the fat over during the cooking. When they are tender remove from the pan with a perforated spoon and fill with a *beurre bourguignonne*, made as follows:

Chop the mushroom stalks very finely and mash them with a fork. Simmer them carefully in a covered saucepan. Leave to get cold, then mix this purée with 4–6 oz. softened butter and add to it 2 tablespoons parsley, a clove of garlic, 2 shallots (all finely chopped), a little salt and plenty of pepper.

Arrange the filled mushrooms in a flat dish with any butter remaining, and heat in a medium oven.

Entrecôte Bercy

An entrecôte proper is cut from the ribs. One good steak is enough for two people. Grill the meat 6–8 minutes on the first side and 3–4 on the second. (This will give you a medium rare steak.) While the meat is cooking, prepare the sauce as follows:

Chop finely three shallots and put into a saucepan with 6 tablespoons dry white wine, a pinch of salt, and freshly milled pepper. Reduce by two-thirds, then beat in quickly 3 oz butter, chopped parsley and a dash of lemon juice. Remove from the heat before the butter becomes too runny, pour over the entrecôtes and serve immediately on a dish garnished with watercress.

Poirat

This is a delicious sweet from the Berry.

Peel a pound of not too ripe pears, cut them into quarters and core them. Lay them in a shallow dish, sprinkle them with 4 tablespoons caster sugar and a liqueur glass of cognac.

Now make a pastry case by first sieving 8 rounded tablespoons plain flour into a basin; press a hole in the middle and pour into it ¼ lb. butter, which you have melted in a double saucepan, and to which you have added 3 tablespoons tepid water. Work this paste as quickly as possible, first with a wooden spoon, then with your hands. Form into a ball, which should not stick to your fingers.

Now roll it on a floured board into a rectangle of roughly 15 in. × 9 in. Arrange the pears in the middle, reserving the juice. Fold the edges of the pastry towards the middle, leaving an opening at the centre. Place on a greased baking sheet and cook in a fairly hot oven for 40 minutes.

Five minutes before dishing pour through the opening of your tart a small carton of cream mixed with the reserved pear juice. On taking the Poirat from the oven, allow it to cool before attempting to detach it from the baking sheet. Use a large slice and slide it on to the serving dish. It should be served cold.

MENU 2

Fish pâté

Mash in a basin an 8-oz. tin of tunny fish with ¼ lb. steamed whiting (or other suitable white fish, such as fresh haddock). When well broken down add 2 tablespoons olive oil, ¼ lb. butter, the juice of half a lemon and a tablespoon of brandy.

Continue mashing until the mixture looks creamy and perfectly amalgamated. Press well into a soufflé dish and leave to set in the refrigerator.

Filets de porc aux fines herbes

A fillet of pork usually weighs about 12 oz., so two should be ample for four people.

Split the fillets lengthways, open them out and beat flat. Lay on them slices of unsmoked bacon to cover completely. Sprinkle with parsley, thyme, marjoram and a few leaves of rosemary. Fold the fillets over and lay in an ovenproof dish. Pour olive oil over the fillets and roast for 30 minutes in a fairly hot oven.

In the meantime cook some rice (a heaped tablespoon per person and a couple more for second helpings). When cooked (about 12 minutes) drain well, and rinse under cold water, arrange in a serving dish and put to dry for 5 minutes in the oven. To serve, cut the fillets in slices, lay them on the rice and pour the juices over.

MENU 3

Gratin d'aubergines

Choose small aubergines and do not peel them. Slice them fairly thickly and cook for 5 minutes in boiling salted water. Aubergines are a very watery vegetable (like their first cousins, vegetable marrows) so be sure to drain them thoroughly. You can leave them in a colander while you are making the sauce.

For four people chop a small onion and cook it, without allowing it to colour, in a mixture of oil and butter. Add 1 lb. of coarsely chopped tomatoes; season with salt, freshly ground pepper, chopped parsley and a little dried basil. Cook slowly, uncovered, till the tomatoes are reduced to a thick pulp. Sieve this sauce back into the pan and leave at the side of the stove.

Now arrange the aubergines in a shallow dish and pour the

sauce over. (If the sauce looks too runny, first reduce it over heat for a minute or two.) Sprinkle with breadcrumbs, chopped parsley, and a little oil, and cook uncovered in a slow oven for about an hour. You can eat it hot or cold.

Pigeonneaux en cocotte

You must buy young roasting pigeons for this dish, and allow one bird per person. Brown the birds in butter and arrange them in an ovenproof dish with a lid. Add a little more butter to the melted fat in the pan and sauté 2 medium-sized onions, thinly sliced, and 4 carrots cut into rounds. Put a *bouquet* of parsley, thyme and bay leaf in with the vegetables, cover, and leave to steam in the pan till they have softened a little.

Now cover the pigeons with half the vegetables, and dispose the rest between the birds. Season with salt and pepper, and pour over 3 tablespoons brandy and the same quantity of melted butter. Lay a piece of foil over the top of the dish and cover with the lid. Cook in a fairly hot oven for 35–40 minutes. Serve in the casserole.

MENU 4

Cornets de jambon fourrés

You must buy circular slices of ham for this, and they must be sliced thin enough to fold. Form each slice into a cone and fill with well-beaten *mousse de volaille*. In France and many other Continental countries this can be bought at any good char-cuterie, but if you are unable to buy it, make it as follows:

Boil a small chicken with an onion, a carrot, a clove of garlic, a strip of lemon peel, some bacon rinds, a few parsley stalks, a bay leaf, a sprig of thyme and the giblets of the bird except the liver. Season with salt and freshly milled black pepper and simmer till absolutely tender. Then skin it,

112

remove the flesh from the bones, chop finely and pound. Cook the liver of the bird for a minute or two in butter, add a tablespoon of brandy and set light to it. When the flame is extinguished add the liver and its juices to the chicken and pound till well amalgamated. Check the seasoning and stir in a level dessertspoon of gelatine diluted in ¼ pint of strained stock, then a carton of thick cream well whipped. Leave in a cool place till beginning to set, then fold in the stiffly beaten whites of 2 eggs. Keep in the refrigerator till wanted.

Arrange the cones on a flat dish and serve very cold, decorated with rounds of hard-boiled egg and chopped parsley.

Veau St Emilion

Brown 2 lb. stewing veal for 5 minutes in half a tumbler of oil. Sprinkle a tablespoon of flour over the meat, stir well with a wooden spoon till amalgamated, then add half a tumbler of red Bordeaux and an equal amount of water. Season with salt, pepper and tarragon. Stir well, lower the heat, cover and gently simmer on an asbestos mat for an hour and a half.

While the meat is cooking, boil 2 eggs for 10 minutes, put into cold water for a moment and then shell them. Pass them through the medium mesh of a food mill.

Arrange the meat in the serving dish, pour over the sauce and sprinkle with the sieved eggs.

Serve with *pommes mousseline* (a very creamy purée of potatoes).

Gâteau de fromage blanc

Put the yolks of 2 eggs into the top of a double boiler. Add 2 tablespoons castor sugar, 3 dessertspoons powdered gelatine, ½ pint orange juice (this should be made from fresh oranges), and a pinch of salt, and simmer till the gelatine is dissolved. In the meantime sieve ½ lb. cream cheese (Gervais or Petits Suisses are suitable if you cannot find any by the pound) with a fork. Stir the mixture in the saucepan and when thickened like a custard remove from heat and add to the sieved cheese. It should look rather like a cake mixture. Now add a dessertspoon grated orange peel and $\frac{1}{2}$ pint stiffly-whipped cream. Whisk the egg whites into peaks, then add 2 tablespoons sugar. Whisk again till stiff, then fold into the cheese mixture. Pour into a soufflé dish or tin rinsed with cold water, and chill in the fridge. To serve, turn out on a flat dish, and decorate with grated biscuit crumbs (digestive biscuits are excellent).

MENU 5

Saucisses en pâté

For the pastry rub 4 Petits Suisses and half their weight of butter into half their combined weight of flour. Leave to rest for an hour.

Spread 6 tablespoons French mustard over 6 sausages, and roll each one into a piece of pastry. Pinch the ends and make sure the seam along the length of the sausage is well closed. Lay the sausages on a lightly floured baking sheet and cook in a hot oven for 20 minutes.

Chou rouge à l'étuvée

Remove the tough outside leaves of a small red cabbage, cut into quarters and cut out the white stalk. Slice the cabbage thinly and arrange in an ovenproof dish in layers alternately with sliced onions and cooking apples peeled, cored and sliced. Season the layers with salt, pepper and sugar. Place a *bouquet* of parsley, thyme, bay leaf and a piece of orange peel in the middle and pour over 2 tablespoons of sweet sherry, or port, and the same amount of wine vinegar. Cover the dish and cook very slowly (about $2\frac{1}{2}$–3 hours) in a slow oven.

You can prepare this dish a day in advance, as it re-heats very successfully.

Baked apples

Choose Bramleys for preference. Leave the skins on and remove the cores. Fill the cavities with a paste made of 2 oz.
butter, 2 oz. brown sugar, ½ teaspoon ground cinnamon and
nutmeg mixed with a teaspoon of grated lemon peel. Arrange
in a shallow dish, pour over a tablespoon of lemon juice
and the same amount of water, and bake in a moderate oven
for 40 minutes.

MENU 6

Soufflé Parmentier

Peel 1½ lb. floury potatoes and cut into large pieces. Wash well
and put into cold salted water. Bring to the boil and cook
gently till soft enough to pass easily through the finest mesh
of a food mill. When you have done this, check the seasoning
and add pepper and a good grating of nutmeg. Now beat in a
small carton of cream, mix well, then add, one by one, the
yolks of 3 eggs. Whip the whites into stiff peaks and fold them
into the purée. Butter a soufflé dish and gently pour in the
mixture. Place in the middle of a pre-heated fairly hot oven,
and bake for 30 minutes. The soufflé is ready when it begins to
detach itself from the sides of the mould, and the top is well
browned.

Serve with a *coulis de tomates*, a thick tomato sauce (prepared as in *Gratin d'aubergines* (Menu 3)).

Coquilles St Jacques à la Côte d'Argent

Allow 2 or 3 scallops per person.

Melt an ounce of butter in a pan and gently cook 2 shallots
or small onions. Clean the scallops and remove the membrane
and the black pocket. Cut the scallops in half and add to the
shallots in the frying-pan. Pour over a small glass of dry white

wine and season with a little salt. Bring to the boil, cover, and simmer gently for 8 minutes. While the fish is cooking, melt some butter in a saucepan and sauté ¼ lb. mushrooms thinly sliced lengthways.

Take 4 half scallop shells and arrange a layer of mushrooms on each, then place the scallops on top, making sure that each person has an equal share of red and white meat.

For the sauce, melt 2 oz. butter, add a rounded tablespoon flour and mix well. Add the mushroom liquid and any left over from cooking the scallops, bring gently to the boil, stirring all the while, and simmer for a few minutes. Now add 2 tablespoons cream and a tablespoon grated cheese. Stir well again and pour over the fish.

Put in a hot oven to brown for 10 minutes. Serve at once.

Ananas au Kirsch

Use preferably a fresh pineapple. Slice into rounds, peel them and remove the hard centre core. Sprinkle with white sugar and about 2 tablespoons Kirschwasser.

Smoked cod's roe

Buy the roe in a piece and allow your guests to help themselves. The skin is rather tough, so make sure you have a sharp knife, Serve with quarters of lemon, and hot slices of toast, with butter served separately.

Tajine aux raisins secs (a North African dish)

The night before you intend cooking this dish, put ½ lb. seedless raisins to soak. Remove the fat from 2 lb. of stewing lamb or mutton, cut the meat into large-sized chunks and put them into a saucepan, just covered with cold water. Add a small piece of root ginger finely grated (or a pinch if you only have the powdered variety), $\frac{1}{2}$ teaspoon saffron, a good pinch of cinnamon, a tablespoon of caster sugar, salt and pepper. Cover and cook very gently on the top of the stove for 2 hours. Now take out the pieces of meat, drain them well and lay them in a fireproof dish. Add the strained raisins and 1 lb. sliced onions to the liquid in the saucepan, cover and simmer for a further half hour. Pour the sauce over the meat, sprinkle with a tablespoon of caster sugar and put in a hot oven for 10 minutes to brown. Serve with a bowl of plainly boiled rice.

MENU 8

Asparagus. Sauce mousseline froide

Tie the asparagus into little bundles and cook in slightly salted water until tender. (Use a small enough saucepan to enable you to stand the asparagus upright so that the tips are out of the water; as they are more tender than the stalks, this prevents them from getting over-cooked and disintegrating.) Allow to cool on a cloth.

For the sauce make a mayonnaise with lemon juice instead of vinegar, and just before serving add some whipped cream. This makes the sauce deliciously light.

Gigot à la provençale

Pour the following marinade over a leg of lamb:

4 tablespoons olive oil; the juice of 2 lemons; tarragon, basil, 3 bay leaves, a few sprigs of parsley, thyme, a clove of garlic, all minced together; salt and 6 peppercorns. Leave all at least a couple of hours, turning the meat over from time to time.

Remove the meat from the marinade and roast in the usual way, allowing about 20 minutes to the pound.

Serve with a lightly dressed salad and a *sauce à la ciboulette*. For this beat together $\frac{1}{2}$ lb. sieved cottage cheese, and a small carton of cream. Add salt, pepper and a pinch of paprika. Stir a tablespoon of chopped chives into the sauce just before serving.

Galette aux abricots

Soak ½ lb. dried apricots in water for two or three hours, then stew them slowly in the water in which they have soaked. When soft, strain the juice and put the fruit through a sieve. Transfer the purée to a saucepan and add ¼ lb. butter, 2 oz. sugar, and the yolks of 4 eggs. Keep the heat low and stir till the mixture is amalgamated and creamy. Allow to cool. In the meantime whip the whites of the eggs into stiff peaks, and fold carefully into the purée.

Butter a soufflé dish, pour in the mixture, and steam for 45–50 minutes. It should set rather like a custard. Allow to go cold, before decorating the top with slivers of almonds. Serve with a separate sauce made from a carton of cream thinned with some of the apricot juice.

MENU 9

Quiche Lorraine

Make a *pâte brisé* with ½ lb. flour, ¼ lb. butter, 3 tablespoons water, ½ teaspoon salt. Work the pastry quickly with your hands, knead it into a ball and leave to rest in the cool for at least 2 hours. When required roll it out thinly and line a flan tin with it. Prick the base with a fork. Cut some streaky bacon into narrow strips and lay them on the pastry. Scatter ½ oz. butter in tiny pieces over the bacon. Beat together half a pint of cream with 3 eggs, season with freshly milled black pepper and a pinch of salt, and put carefully over the bacon. Scatter another ½ oz. butter in little pieces on the top and bake in a hot oven for 20 minutes. Take a look, and if it is brown and risen like a soufflé, lower the heat and cook for a further 10 minutes, when the custard should be set. Serve at once.

Canard à la normande

In a large fireproof casserole melt a little butter and sauté 4 rashers of streaky bacon cut into dice. Add a large onion, sliced, and 2 carrots, cut into rounds. Allow the onions and carrots to soften before placing the duck on the bed of vegetables. Pour a little stock over the bird, check the seasoning, sprinkle a tablespoon of sugar over, cover the dish and simmer till tender, turning the duck two or three times during the cooking. In the meantime make some apple purée. When ready to serve, fry some slices of bread in butter, spread them thickly with the apple purée, carve the duck and place each piece on a slice of bread. Pour over the sauce from the cooking, arrange the vegetables in the dish and hand round some more purée in a sauceboat.

Petits pois à la française (young green peas cooked in butter with shredded lettuce heart and spring onions) can be served at the same time.

MENU IO

Flan de courgettes

Choose as small courgettes as possible; for four people you will need 1 lb. They should be young enough for you to leave the skins on. Slice into rounds about ¼ inch thick, and blanch them for 7 minutes in boiling salted water to which you have added a *bouquet garni* (parsley, thyme and bay leaf). Drain well, then spread a layer of courgettes in a shallow fireproof dish, sprinkle with a tablespoon of grated cheese, cover with the remaining courgettes and finish with another tablespoon of cheese. Now beat together 3 eggs with half a pint of milk, salt and pepper. Pour this over the courgettes. Cook for 25-30 minutes in a slow oven till set.

Rôti de porc chasseur

For four people buy a piece of loin of pork weighing about 1½ lb. and get the butcher to chine it. Heat 3 tablespoons olive oil in a heavy pan and brown the meat all over. Warm a tablespoon of brandy in a ladle, set it alight and pour while flaming over the meat; shake the pan to make sure that the brandy reaches every part of the meat. Sprinkle the joint with a tablespoon of flour, moisten with half a pint of warm water, then add two-thirds of a bottle of Burgundy or Côtes du Rhône a *bouquet garni*, salt and pepper. Cover and simmer for three-quarters of an hour. Now add 6 small whole onions and half a clove of garlic finely chopped. Cook for another half hour. The liquid should have reduced by at least half, and the sauce should have become smooth and shiny.

Serve with *haricots verts*, plainly boiled, and tossed in butter and a powdering of parsley finely chopped.

Gooseberry cheese

Cook a pound of young gooseberries with 4 tablespoons sugar and 2 tablespoons water till soft. Put through the finest mesh of the food mill. Beat up ½ lb. cream cheese (unsalted) with a tablespoon of caster sugar, and allow to drain through muslin for an hour or so in a cool place. When ready to serve, beat the cheese and gooseberries together till perfectly amalgamated, and mix in a carton of double cream.

MENU II

Tomates Babua

Heat 2 tablespoons of oil and 2 oz. butter in a fireproof dish. When they are well amalgamated, lightly brown 2 medium-sized sliced onions. Now lay on top of the onions 1½ lb. tomatoes cut in halves. (Leave the skins on, as they will add to the flavour.) Cook the tomatoes, cut side down, for 5 minutes or so, then turn them over and allow to simmer for another quarter of an hour. While the vegetables are cooking, work 2 level tablespoons flour into a small carton of cream until you get a smooth paste. A few minutes before serving, pour this mixture in between the tomatoes, add salt and pepper, and mix gently with the wrong end of a wooden spoon, in order not to disarrange the tomatoes. Serve sprinkled with plenty of freshly chopped parsley.

Terrine de poulet

You will need a boiling chicken weighing 2½ lb., ¼ lb. bacon, 6 oz. lean ham, a few fragments of truffle, 6 oz. mushrooms, 6 oz. sausage meat, a calf's (or pig's) foot, brandy, one or two carrots, and an onion. Remove the giblets from the bird and reserve. Cut the chicken in conveniently-sized joints and brown them in butter with the bacon cut into dice. Season with pepper and cook uncovered for another 30 minutes.

While the chicken is cooking make the forcemeat by chopping the liver, the gizzard, the heart and the pieces of truffle as small as possible, together with the ham.

Finely slice the mushrooms and cook them in another pan in a little butter, then add the chopped giblets, truffle and ham and sausage meat.

When the pieces of chicken are more or less cooked, drain them and cut the flesh from the bones in slices as near the same size as possible. Remove the rest of the meat, mince it and add to the giblet and sausage mixture.

Now spread in a terrine alternate layers of chicken and forcemeat, sprinkle with a little brandy, and lay on the top of the pâté a bay leaf and strips of fat bacon arranged in a criss-cross pattern. Cover with foil and the lid of the terrine, place in a tin with a little water and cook in a moderate oven for up to 3 hours. Look at it after 2 hours, and if it shows signs of detaching itself from the sides of the terrine, it is done.

While the pâté is cooking, simmer the carcass of the bird, the carrots and onion, and the calf's foot in salted water for the same length of time. Strain this stock.

Prick the pâté all over with a skewer and trickle the reduced and concentrated stock into the holes. Leave to cool overnight with a weight on top. Serve either in or out of the dish, with a salad of lettuce hearts.

Strawberry mousse

Lighter than ice cream, this makes the perfect ending to a summer meal.

Pass 1 lb. ripe strawberries through a sieve. Beat into the pulp 6 oz. well-sieved icing sugar. When completely amalgamated, whisk an egg white till stiff and fold into the purée.

Chill and serve in individual glasses.

MENU 12

Concombres aux crevettes

First make a very mustardy mayonnaise with lemon juice instead of vinegar. Cut the cucumbers into chunks about 2 inches long and hollow out the centres; you can do this with an apple corer. Now mix peeled prawns with the mayonnaise, and fill the pieces of cucumber. Pile up on a dish and garnish with whole prawns and slices of lemon.

Roast chicken

Remove the giblets and put a good piece of butter into the bird. Rub the outside with salt and lemon juice and spread more butter over the breast and joints. Put half a lemon into the bird. Roast in a hot oven, basting frequently. If the breast seems cooked before the thighs, cover it with foil. Carve into neat joints, arrange on a dish and lay bunches of watercress at each end. Serve the juices in a sauceboat.

Coeurs à la crème

These small cream cheeses are served as a sweet in France, sprinkled with sugar and accompanied by thick fresh cream. You can make do instead with Fontainebleau or Chambourcy. Serve separately a bowl of fresh strawberries.

MENU 13

Cassolettes aux champignons

Clean and wash 1 lb. mushrooms and slice them lengthwise, leaving the stalks on. Dry them carefully, then put them into a saucepan with the juice of half a lemon, a medium-sized onion thinly sliced, a *bouquet garni*, salt, pepper and a wineglass of water. Cover and cook gently for a quarter of an hour, then drain off any liquid that has not evaporated. Remove the *bouquet* and add, away from the fire, 4 eggs well beaten, the juice of half a lemon and a small carton of cream. Make sure that the eggs are perfectly amalgamated with the other ingredients. Pour the mixture into individual fireproof dishes and set them in a shallow pan half filled with water. Cover the pan and simmer for half an hour. Cool. As this dish is eaten cold, it can be made the day before.

Homard à l'américaine

This is a dish for a great occasion, but it will amply repay the trouble and expense. For four people you will need two freshly boiled lobsters weighing 2 lb. each. Get your fishmonger to split them in half. Remove the meat from the shells and claws and cook for a few minutes in 6 tablespoons olive oil. Add 6 shallots chopped finely. Heat 2 tablespoons brandy in a ladle, set it alight and pour over the fish. Flame for half a minute, then add half a bottle of dry white wine, and allow to bubble for a minute or two. Lower the heat and stir in 2 tablespoons tomato purée, herbs and a tiny pinch of cayenne pepper. Bring slowly to the boil and simmer for 20 minutes, not longer, as lobster becomes tough if cooked too long. Remove the pieces of fish, drain well and keep them warm.

Reduce the sauce by simmering it for another 15–20 minutes. Taste, and if necessary add salt. Remove the creamy parts of the lobster from the shells and add to the sauce, with ½ teaspoon saffron, and cook for a further 5 minutes.

Arrange the pieces of lobster in their half shells on a dish. Mix a small carton of cream with the sauce (which must not boil again), and pour over the fish.

Sprinkle with chopped parsley and serve at once.

Raspberry and red-currant tart

Make a *pâte brisé* with ½ lb. flour, ¼ lb. butter, an egg, a pinch of salt and 3 tablespoons white sugar. Work the paste quickly, and lightly roll it on a floured cloth, so that you can turn it without too much handling into a sandwich tin about 10 inches across. Prick the base with a fork and fill the centre with dried beans. Bake in a moderate oven for 20 minutes. When cooked, remove the beans and leave the tart to cool.

Cook 1½ lb. firm raspberries and ½ lb. red-currants with 6 oz. white sugar (no water) for a few minutes. Strain carefully, in order not to break the fruit, and fill the tart. Put the juice into a pan with a tablespoon of red-currant jelly. Warm and stir till the syrup has thickened. Then pour it over the cooled fruit. Serve cold.

Gâteau d'épinards

Wash 1½ lb. spinach in several waters, drain in a colander and put into a saucepan with a nut of butter. Cook gently until most of the liquid has dried out.

In the meantime make 4 little omelettes of an egg each. Lay each one in a separate saucer.

Make ½ pint of very thick béchamel sauce, and add to it 6 oz. grated cheese and ¼ lb. streaky bacon cut into small cubes. Remove the spinach from the heat, and mix well with the sauce. Beat in, one at a time, two whole eggs. Check the seasoning.

Butter a soufflé dish and lay an omelette at the bottom, then a layer of the spinach mixture. Continue with alternate layers of omelette and spinach, finishing with an omelette. Cover the dish with foil, and put into a pre-heated hot oven for half an hour.

You can serve this either as it is, or unmould it on to a plate.

Rognons de veau au vin blanc

For four people allow two veal kidneys. Remove the membranes and slice. Sauté the pieces in butter over a fairly high flame, then take them out with a perforated slice and set aside. Add ¼ lb. mushrooms, sliced lengthways, to the butter and cook them until the butter is nearly all absorbed. Pour a wineglassful of white wine into the pan and stir hard with a wooden spoon in order to detach all the particles and juices adhering to the pan. Now stir in a teaspoonful of Dijon mustard and a small carton of cream. When thickened, add a couple of drops of brandy. Arrange the kidneys in a dish, check seasoning in the sauce and pour it over the kidneys. Serve immediately.

Spaghetti Napolitaine

Have ready a large pan full of boiling salted water and add
¼ lb. spaghetti per person. Keep the water boiling fast and stir
the pasta from time to time so that it does not stick. While it is
cooking, make a sauce as follows. Pour a film of olive oil over
the bottom of a frying-pan. When hot, slip in 2 cloves of
sliced garlic and let them cook for a few seconds. Add half a
dozen ripe tomatoes roughly chopped. Season with salt,
pepper and a pinch of dried basil. Drain the spaghetti, arrange
in a serving dish, pour the sauce over, and serve with a bowl of
grated Parmesan cheese.

Jambon sous la cendre

Spread slices of cooked ham with pâté de foie and lay one on
top of the other. Brush a piece of greaseproof paper with oil
and lay on it the slices of ham. Fold over the paper so that you
have a hermetically sealed parcel. Put in a moderate oven and
bake for 20 minutes.

In the meantime make a *sauce madère*. Melt 1½ oz. butter in a
saucepan and add a heaped tablespoon of flour. Allow to
colour deeply. Add little by little a glass and a half of white
wine, salt, pepper and a *bouquet garni*. Stir well and cook gently
for 25 minutes. Just before serving remove the *bouquet* and add
3 tablespoons Madeira. Unpack the ham at the table, and serve
the sauce separately.

Les Acrats (Beignets Martiniquais)

You can make these either with cod or prawns, or a mixture of
the two. While you are preparing the batter for the beignets
leave the fish to macerate in lemon juice.

For 4–6 people you will need ½ lb. fish. Mix ½ lb. flour with equal quantities of water and milk (about 6–8 tablespoons in all). Beat well and leave for at least an hour. If you can leave overnight, so much the better. Pound the fish and season with thyme, bay leaf, parsley, salt and pepper. Chop finely a large onion and a small pimento (taking care to remove all the seeds) and add all to the batter. Correct the seasoning.

Drop the mixture in spoonfuls into very hot oil. When the beignets are golden and crisp, drain on kitchen paper and keep warm in a cool oven with the door open.

Escalopes de veau à la rennaise

Brown the escalopes in butter and oil, together with a whole clove of garlic and 2 tablespoons chopped onion. Make sure that the meat is evenly browned all over, then add 2 tablespoons tomato purée and a tumbler of white wine. Cover the pan and simmer gently for an hour, preferably on an asbestos mat. Remove the meat and keep warm. Now add to the sauce 3 tablespoons Madeira. Put 2 tablespoons brandy into a ladle, warm, and set alight and pour flaming into the sauce. Leave to simmer for a further 30 minutes, adding if necessary a little more white wine or stock.

Arrange the meat on a dish. Add 2 or 3 tablespoons thick cream to the sauce before pouring over the meat. Sprinkle with finely chopped parsley, and place round the edge of the dish croutons fried crisply in oil.

MENU 17

Oeufs en meurette ménagère

This version of one of the most famous of Burgundian dishes was given to me by the chef of the *Restaurant du Châpeau Rouge* at Dijon. The richness of the sauce makes it very suitable as a main luncheon dish, when you should allow 2 eggs per person. As a sumptuous introduction to a dinner it should be followed by a roast or grill.

For four people bring half a bottle of Beaujolais, or a light Burgundy, to the boil. Add a crushed clove of garlic, a chopped onion and a *bouquet garni*. Turn down the heat and cook gently, uncovered, for 10 minutes.

In the meantime fry some slices of bread very crisply in olive oil. Drain on paper and keep aside.

Continue to reduce the sauce to a third of its original volume and thicken it with a liaison of *beurre manié* (work $\frac{1}{2}$ oz. butter with a level tablespoon of flour until they are amalgamated to a smooth paste; you will find this is easiest if you do it with a fork. Add to the sauce and stir gently). Season with salt and pepper and leave to simmer for a further 10 minutes. In another saucepan sauté some little onions (the kind used for pickling), or shallots if you can get them, and a couple of rashers of bacon cut into cubes. Add to the sauce and leave to cook for another 10 minutes.

Poach the eggs, drain them well, arrange in a dish, and strain the sauce over. Put the pieces of fried bread around the dish, powder with finely chopped parsley and serve immediately.

N.B.—Do not poach the eggs in one of those contraptions which harden the whites to a custard-like consistency. They should be cooked in barely shuddering water with a few drops of vinegar, and the whites should enrobe the yolks.

Grilled lamb chops with braised celery

Just a reminder that lamb should not be overcooked; the centre of the chops should remain pink. Serve with braised celery. For four people buy 2 heads of celery, cut off the hard end and wash the sticks very thoroughly in cold water. Cut them in half and blanch them in boiling water for 10 minutes.

Drain them, arrange in a fireproof dish, dot well with butter, cover either with a lid or foil and cook in a moderate oven until tender. They will take three-quarters of an hour if young, a further 15 minutes if the outside stalks are tough.

MENU 18

Smoked trout, Horseradish sauce

The trout should be served on individual plates. Allow one per person and supply plenty of lemons cut into quarters.

For the sauce, put a good tablespoon of horseradish into a basin, season with salt and lemon juice, then stir in a carton of thick cream, which you have slightly whipped, and a few drops of olive oil. Transfer to a sauce boat and allow your guests to help themselves.

Roast saddle of young venison

One of the most interesting combinations of food and wine is the piquancy of young game with the spicy white wines of the Rhine. The following recipe was given to me by Herr Michiels, the chef at Deinhard & Co. in Koblenz. A saddle should be enough for eight people.

Prepare it by detaching the meat from either side of the backbone with a sharp knife, then slip wide strips of pork fat (in Germany this is called *speck*) into the pockets. Fold the meat back into place, tie with string (or hold it with elastic bands) and roast in a fairly hot oven, allowing about 12 to 15 minutes per pound. (But don't overcook it—the flesh should be pink and tender when served.)

While the meat is cooking, peel, cut in half, core and poach some pears in a sugar and water syrup; then fill them with a compote of cranberries. In another saucepan melt some butter and sauté ½ lb. mushrooms. If you can get the little orange chanterelles they will give the authentic flavour; otherwise

I

buy the smallest mushrooms you can find and cut them in half. When the mushrooms are half cooked pour half a glass of light red wine into the pan and leave to simmer. Reduce the sauce and add to it 2 tablespoons cream.

To serve, put the joint on a dish, remove the string and carve in slices, cutting downwards from the backbone. Pour the sauce over, and arrange the cranberry-filled pear halves round the dish.

The traditional accompaniment to this dish is *pommes croquettes*. Cook 1 lb. floury potatoes till soft enough to pass through a sieve. Add butter and milk to make a purée stiff enough to roll into balls. Dip these in beaten egg, roll in dried breadcrumbs and fry in very hot oil.

MENU 19

Gratin de soles

For four people it is best to make this dish with a large sole weighing about 1¾ lb. There will be less waste of bones and heads. Otherwise allow one sole, weighing about ½ lb., per person.

Clean the fish and remove both skins, or get the fishmonger to do it for you. Chop finely 2 shallots, ¼ lb. mushrooms, a tablespoon of minced parsley and chives. Spread over the base of an oval fireproof dish 1½ oz. butter worked with the same quantity of flour, add salt and pepper, sprinkle with stale breadcrumbs and lay the sole on this bed. Pour over 6 tablespoons white sine with an equal quantity of water (or stock). Simmer on the top of the stove for about 10 minutes, then transfer to the oven (Reg. 5) and leave for a further quarter of an hour (for individual fish), 20 minutes for one large one. Serve in the same dish.

Gnocchis romanais

Boil together 9 tablespoons water, 2 oz. butter and a pinch

130

each of salt, pepper and nutmeg. As soon as the liquid has come to the boil add, all at once, ¼ lb. flour. Beat it in with a wooden spoon until the mixture shrinks from the sides of the pan and forms an elastic ball. Remove from heat, leave to cool, then break an egg into the paste. Continue beating till the egg is thoroughly amalgamated, add another in the same manner, and then a third. Lastly beat in 3 oz. grated cheese. Now spread the paste about ½ inch thick on to a floured tin, and leave to go cold. When you are ready to cook the gnocchis, cut the paste, with a sharp knife dipped in water, into little squares. Drop them into boiling salted water, a few at a time because they puff up, and cook for 8–10 minutes. Drain well and run the strainer under the cold tap for a moment to firm up the gnocchis. Drain again, arrange in a dish, put in a cool oven while you prepare a *coulis de tomates* (see page 115). Pour over the sauce just before serving.

Compôte d'automne

If you can lay your hands on a couple of pounds of quinces, this unusual mixture of fruits makes a lovely finish to a dinner party where the previous courses have been particularly satisfying.

Peel and core the quinces and cut them into large pieces. Lay them in a saucepan with half a tumbler of cold water, and sprinkle them with sugar (about 4 tablespoons). Cover, and cook slowly for 15 minutes, then remove the lid and cook for a further 15 minutes.

Turn into a glass dish, leave to cool, and cover with a mixture of black and white grapes.

MENU 20

Moules à la crème

I have included this classic Normandy dish because mussels are one of the most ingratiating accompaniments to crisp, delicate white wines. Although mussels are eaten all the way along the west coast of France, the best to me are the small ones found along the fringes of the English Channel. The smaller the mussels, the more delicate the flavour. In any case this is not a dish to be eaten at a distance from the smell of the sea.

The following recipe was given to me by Monsieur Guy Hellebruyck, formerly *chef de cuisine* at the famous restaurant *La Tour d'Argent* in Paris, now director of the *Restaurant de la Gare Maritime* in Boulogne, which in spite of its name is an elegant setting for really first-class and imaginative food. I remember an hors d'oeuvre of cold cauliflower redeemed from its usual mediocrity by being tossed in a golden-red sauce spiced with paprika. The important part of the following recipe is the use of mignonnette pepper (coarse-ground white peppercorns) which gives a particularly piquant flavour to the sauce.

Allow 1 pint of mussels per person. Clean and wash in several waters and remove the beards. Throw the mussels into a saucepan without any other liquid, and cook over a fierce heat till they have opened. Throw away any which have not opened or have a broken shell. Strain the liquid at the bottom of the saucepan through a clean muslin and put into a clean saucepan. Add a wineglass of dry white wine, a *bouquet garni*, plenty of mignonnette pepper, a good tablespoon of finely chopped onion, shallot and parsley, and an ounce of butter. Reduce a little.

Empty a carton of double cream into another pan and cook gently till it thickens. In the meantime remove the empty half-shells of the mussels. Now combine the cream with the reduced liquid, arrange the mussels in a deep dish, pour the sauce over, sprinkle with parsley and serve at once.

Noix de veau au citron

Grate into a saucepan enough suet (preferably kidney) to sauté the piece of veal. The *noix* corresponds to the 'topside'.

Get your butcher to tie it into a neat shape. Brown the meat in the melted fat and season with salt, pepper, cinnamon and nutmeg. When the meat is golden all over add 2 table-spoons water, cover the pan and simmer for an hour. At this point add to the juices in the pan the juice of 2 lemons and leave to simmer for a further half hour.

Put the joint on a dish and serve with the juices poured over it.

Serve with *endives braisées*, allowing 2 endives (in England usually known as chicory) per person. Wipe them clean and lay them in a buttered fireproof dish. Dot with small pieces of butter, and pour over a little of the juice from the meat. Cover and cook in a slow oven for about 1½ hours.

Crêpes Suzette

You can make these pancakes the day before you want to eat them. If you keep them flat on a plate covered with foil you can re-heat them perfectly satisfactorily by setting the plate over a saucepan of hot water and letting them warm through.

For the batter put 8 rounded tablespoons plain flour into a basin with a teaspoon of salt. Stir in 2 tablespoons of oil and 2 eggs. Beat well, then add half a pint of milk and water in equal quantities. Continue beating (I usually use an egg whisk at this point). Strain into a clean basin, cover and leave in the cool for at least 2 hours.

When you are ready to cook the pancakes, run a few drops of oil over the bottom of a frying-pan, heat to just under boiling point, then with a ladle or large spoon quickly pour in a thin layer of batter. Tilt the pan so that the surface is evenly covered, cook for a minute or two, then with a palette knife turn the pancake over and fry the other side.

Now for the sauce. In a tepid bowl cream 2 oz. butter with the juice of 2 oranges, 3 tablespoons Grand Marnier or Cointreau, a teaspoon of grated orange peel and 5 tablespoons caster sugar. Brush each pancake with this cream, roll them, lay them in a shallow dish and sprinkle with sugar. Heat a ladleful of brandy, set it alight and pour flaming over the pancakes.

Serve at once.

(You can fill the pancakes and put covered to keep warm before you start your meal, and flambé them at the last minute, even at the table.)

MENU 21

Soufflé au fromage

Make a béchamel sauce by melting an ounce of butter in a saucepan; stir into it an ounce of flour and continue stirring till smooth; gradually add half a pint of milk, and stir till thickened and amalgamated. This will take about 10 minutes. Now add 2 oz. grated Parmesan (or Gruyère if you prefer its slightly sweet taste), salt, plenty of freshly ground pepper, and a scrape of nutmeg. Remove from the heat and beat in, one at a time, the yolks of 3 eggs.

Pre-heat the oven (gas Reg. 6 is about right) and butter a soufflé dish. Whisk the whites of the eggs till stiff and creamy and fold them gently into the béchamel mixture, turning carefully so that the combination appears light and spongy. Put into the oven for 25 minutes, when the top should be brown and the inside still creamy. Serve immediately.

Oison au chou

To achieve the most satisfactory result you must choose a young goose before it has grown too fat.

Cut the bird into joints and brown in butter in a large pan. (Ideally this dish should be cooked on top of the stove but if you do not have a large enough pan, cook it in the oven.) Lower the heat, cover the pan and cook gently for 40–45 minutes.

In the meantime blanch a white cabbage in boiling salted water for 10 minutes. Drain well and remove the leaves. Now take the pieces of goose out of the pan and lay the cabbage leaves in the juices which have come out of the bird. Lay the pieces of bird on top, cover and simmer for a further half hour.

Serve very hot with a not too sweet purée of apples.

MENU 22

Omelette Médocaine

Nearly every cook will give you his or her own special method of making successful omelettes. Our own cook who 'had a hand' with eggs used to tell me that the secret was to touch the eggs in the pan as little as possible, but to shake the pan continually in order to keep the mixture from sticking. I have found this method absolutely foolproof. Her two other tips were to cover the bottom of the pan with a film of oil before putting in the butter and to remove the omelette to the dish while the centre is still creamy and unset.

The traditional omelette of the Médoc is delicately flavoured with equal quantities of parsley, tarragon and chives, finely chopped but not minced into powder.

Beat the eggs gently with a fork; the white and yolk should be just mixed. Season with salt, freshly ground pepper and the herbs. The average-sized pan (10 inches across) makes an omelette of 3 eggs. The mixture should be run evenly and thinly over the pan. If too thick the outside will be leathery before the inside is cooked.

A three-egg omelette should be enough for two people.

Côtes de mouton au muscat

For this dish choose loin chops and prepare the sauce first.

Saturate two lumps of sugar in wine vinegar and put into a small saucepan. Allow them to caramelize to a light brown, add 4 tablespoons Madeira and 2 finely chopped shallots. Mix 3 teaspoons flour to a cream with water, strain into the sauce, stir well and simmer for a quarter of an hour. When the shallots are soft sieve the sauce into a clean pan and add 6 oz. pipped black grapes. Leave over a very low heat, preferably on an asbestos mat, without allowing to come to the boil.

Sauté the chops in butter. They should take about 6 minutes. Arrange them on a hot dish and pour the sauce around.

Serve with braised celery. (See page 128.)

MENU 23

Salade de lentilles aux chipolatas

Soak 6 oz. brown lentils in cold water overnight. Brown an onion in 2 tablespoons of oil. Add a clove of garlic, a bay leaf, salt, and 2 pints water. Put the strained lentils into this stock, cover and cook gently for 1½–2 hours. They should be soft but not mushy. Drain them well and while they are warm mix them with the following dressing:

Stir salt and freshly ground black pepper into a teaspoon of French mustard, a tablespoon each of wine vinegar and lemon juice, and 4 tablespoons oil. When thickened mix with the lentils. Serve with chipolata sausages grilled and left to get cold. Sprinkle with plenty of chopped parsley.

Roast haunch of wild boar

This method of cooking game can also be very successfully applied to venison and hare. A saddle of pork lends itself to it as well.

With a sharp knife detach the meat from either side of the bone. Mince finely 12 juniper berries, a large bay leaf, 3 or 4 leaves of rosemary, a piece of orange peel and 5 to 6 peppercorns, and rub this powder along the bone. Now pour over half a bottle of red wine—preferably Burgundy—and a quarter of a pint of olive oil. Marinate for 24 hours, turning the meat over three or four times. Drain the meat and roast uncovered in a slow oven, basting frequently with butter.

Most game animals and birds tend to be very dry, so the basting is an important part of the cooking. It should take 2 to 3 hours. Shortly before serving, strain the marinade into a saucepan, add a tablespoon of red-currant jelly, reduce by fast boiling for a minute or two, and pour over the meat. The joint should be carved in slices and reconstituted into its original shape.

It can be accompanied by either a very creamy purée of potatoes or potato croquettes. (See page 130.)

A complete haunch of wild boar weighs about 12 lb., so you can really only consider this dish for a large Christmas party. But it makes an admirable main course on a cold winter's night.

Crème de pistaches

Shell 10 oz. pistachio nuts by plunging them into boiling water. Pound them in a mortar, with 3 heaped tablespoons sugar and a tablespoon of Kirsch (this also makes an excellent winter liqueur). Beat in, one by one, the yolks of 3 eggs and half a pint of fresh cream. Transfer to a double boiler and cook, stirring from time to time, till the mixture has thickened and coats the back of a wooden spoon. Pour into a bowl and chill before serving.

MENU 24

Prawns and olives

Allow 2 oz. unshelled prawns per person and serve them piled in a dish. The olives should fill another dish. Provide plenty of fresh crusty bread and unsalted butter, and allow your guests to help themselves.

If you have individual finger bowls, it is a good idea to provide them (filled with warm water and a slice of lemon). If not, a couple of salad bowls at each end of the table can serve the purpose.

Dinde à la girondine

This method of cooking a turkey makes a very welcome change from the traditional sausage-meat stuffing.

Beat together (for a 10 lb. bird) 6 Petits Suisses with a table-spoon of anisette Marie Brizard, and stuff the crop end. Draw the skin over and tuck it underneath the bird when you set it in the roasting tin. Rub lemon juice over the breast and legs, put a good lump of butter together with half a lemon into the body of the bird, and spread softened butter over the outside. Cover with foil and roast in a slow oven (Reg. 4) for $2\frac{1}{2}$–3 hours.

Serve with young Brussels sprouts or braised celery. (See page 128.)

Mince pies

I would really recommend buying mince pies from a good *patissier*, in the same way as most French households buy the Sunday tart for lunch at the local pastrycook who stays open for the purpose. We believe this branch of cookery is best left to the professionals, though I confess that I remove the lids of my mince pies and sprinkle a few drops of brandy in each one before putting them in the oven to warm them up. However, I understand that in England there are relatively few good *patissiers* and that most people prefer to make their own mince pies, though they may buy the mincemeat. It is clearly unnecessary for me to give a recipe here but don't forget the brandy if you can run to it!

A List of Shippers

Bordeaux

Barton & Guestier
J. Calvet et Cie
Cruse
Cordier
Descases
Alexis Lichine
Mâhler-Besse
Marcel Quancard
Sichel
Schröder & Schuyler

Burgundy

Bouchard Père et Fils
Paul Bouchard
Barton & Guestier
J. Calvet et Cie
Chanson Père et Fils
Drouhin
Geisweiler
Hasenklever
Jaboulet-Vercherre
Louis Jadot
Louis Latour

Burgundy (*cont.*)

Prosper Maufoux
Mommessin
Marcilly Frères
Piat
Pierre Ponnelle
Patriarche
Pasquier Vigne
Ropiteau
Thorin
Charles Vienot

Loire

Remy Pannier
La Ladoucette

Alsace

Dopff
Dopff & Irion
Hugel
Trimbach

Champagne

Bollinger

Champagne (*cont.*)

Veuve Clicquot
Georges Goulet
Charles Heidsieck
Piper Heidsieck
Heidsieck Monopole
Krug
Mumm
Mercier
Möet & Chandon
Lanson
Pol Roger
Pommery & Greno
Perrier Jouet
Roederer
Taittinger

Cognac

Hennessy
Hine
Martell
Otard
Courvoisier
Polignac
Rémy Martin
Salignac
Biscuit Dubouché
Denis Mounié
Exshaw
de Luze
Adet Seward

German Still Wines

Deinhard

German Still Wines (*cont.*)

Langenbach
Hallgarten
Valckenberg
Prüm
G. A. Schmidt
G. W. Thoman
Kendermann
O. W. Loeb
Siegal
Sichel

German Sparkling Wines

Deinhard
Henkell
Langenbach
Kupferberg
Matheus Müller

Sherry

Garvey
Duff Gordon
Mackenzie
Sandeman
Valdespino
Williams & Humbert
Domecq
Gonzales Byass
Harvey

Port

Sandeman
Taylor

Port (*cont.*)

Croft
Cockburn
Dow
Fonseca
Quinta da Noval
Graham
Offley Forrester
Warre

Madeira

Barbeito
Cossart Gordon
Blandy
Leacock
Rutherford & Miles

Italy

Bertoli
Ruffino
Antinori
Bolla
Bertani

Spain

Companhia Vinicola del
  Norte España
Bodegas Bilbainas
La Rioja Alta

Spain (*cont.*)

Bodegas Palacio
Bodegas Franco-Españolas

Portugal

Jose-Maria Fonseca
Carvalho Ribeiro & Fereira
Companhia Vinicola de
  Norte Portugal
Sogrape

Australia

Penfold
Seppelt
Hardy
Lindemann

U.S.A. (California)

Almaden Wineries
Charles Krug
Gallo
Louis Martini
Beaulieu Wineries
Souverain Wineries

Sparkling Wines in Eastern States

Taylor

List of Bordeaux Classed Growths

MEDOC
1855 *classification*

Premiers crus	Communes
Ch. Lafite	Pauillac
Ch. Margaux	Margaux
Ch. Latour	Pauillac
Ch. Haut Brion	Pessac (Graves)

Deuxièmes crus	
Ch. Mouton Rothschild	Pauillac
Ch. Rausan-Ségla	Margaux
Ch. Rauzan-Gassies	Margaux
Ch. Léoville-Lascases	Saint-Julien
Ch. Léoville-Poyferré	Saint-Julien
Ch. Léoville Barton	Saint-Julien
Ch. Dufort-Vivens	Margaux
Ch. Lascombes	Margaux
Ch. Gruaud-Larose	Saint-Julien
Ch. Brane-Cantenac	Cantenac
Ch. Pichon-Longueville	Pauillac
Ch. Pichon-Longueville-Lalande	Pauillac
Ch. Ducru-Beaucaillou	Saint-Julien
Ch. Cos d'Estournel	Saint-Estèphe
Ch. Montrose	Saint-Estèphe

geois (cont.)	Communes
nt	Cantenac
y	Bégadan
rdonne	Blaignan
denne	Saint-Yzans
t-Christoly	Saint-Christoly

SAINT EMILION

1955 Classification

reat Growths

eau Ausone	Clos Fourtet
Cheval Blanc	Ch. Gaffelière-Naudes
Beauséjour	Ch. Magdelaine
Belair	Ch. Pavie
Canon	Ch. Trottevieille
Figeac

A SELECTION OF PRINCIPAL AND LESSER GROWTHS OF SAINT EMILION

Ch. l'Arrósee	Ch. Grand Barrail
Ch. Balestard la Tonnelle	Ch. Grand-Corbin-
Ch. Bergat	Despagne
Ch. Cadet-Bon	Ch. l'Angélus
Ch. Cap-de-Mourlin	Ch. Bellevue
Ch. Chauvin	Ch. Boulerne
Ch. Coudert-Pelletan	Ch. Cadet-Piola
Ch. Coutet	Ch. Canon-la-Gaffelière
Ch. Curé-Bon	Ch. Chapelle-Madeleine
Ch. Dassault	Ch. Corbin
Ch. Fonroque	Ch. Croque-Michotte

Troisièmes crus	Communes
Ch. Kirwan	Cantenac
Ch. Issan	Cantenac
Ch. Lagrange	Saint-Julien
Ch. Langoa	Saint-Julien
Ch. Giscours	Labarde
Ch. Maléscot-Saint-Exupéry	Margaux
Ch. Cantenac-Brown	Cantenac
Ch. Palmer	Cantenac
Ch. Grand La Lagune	Ludon
Ch. Desmirail	Margaux
Ch. Calon Ségur	Saint-Estèphe
Ch. Ferrière	Margaux
Ch. Marquis d'Alèsme-Becker	Margaux
Ch. Boyd Cantenac	Margaux

Quatrièmes crus |
--- | ---
Ch. Saint-Pierre-Sevaistre | Saint-Julien
Ch. Saint-Pierre-Bontemps | Saint-Julien
Ch. Branaire-Ducru | Saint-Julien
Ch. Talbot | Saint-Julien
Ch. Duhart-Milon | Pauillac
Ch. Pouget | Cantenac
Ch. La Tour Carnet | Saint-Laurent
Ch. Rochet | Saint-Estèphe
Ch. Beychevelle | Saint-Julien
Ch. Le Prieuré | Cantenac
Ch. Marquis de Terme | Margaux

Cinquièmes crus |
--- | ---
Ch. Pontet-Canet | Pauillac
Ch. Batailley | Pauillac

Cinquièmes crus (*cont.*)	**Communes**
Ch. Haut-Batailley	Pauillac
Ch. Grand-Puy-Lacoste	Pauillac
Ch. Grand-Puy-Ducasse	Pauillac
Ch. Lynch-Bages	Pauillac
Ch. Lynch-Moussas	Pauillac
Ch. Croizet-Bages	Pauillac
Ch. Dansac	Labarde
Ch. Mouton-d'Armailhacq	Pauillac
(now called Ch. du Baron Philippe)
Ch. du Tertre	Arsac
Ch. Haut-Bages-Libéral	Pauillac
Ch. Pédesclaux	Pauillac
Ch. Belgrave	Saint-Laurent
Ch. Camensac	Saint-Laurent
Ch. Cantemerle	Macau
Ch. Cos Labory	Saint-Estéphe
Ch. Clerc-Milon-Mondon	Pauillac

A SELECTION OF CRUS BOURGEOIS OF THE MÉDOC

Crus Bourgeois	**Communes**
Ch. Angludet	Cantenac
Ch. Beauséjour	Listrac
Ch. Bel-Air	Saint-Estèphe
Ch. Bel-Air-Marquis d'Aligre	Soussans-Margaux
Ch. Belgrave	Saint-Laurent
Ch. Bellegrave	Listrac
Ch. Bellevue	Cussac
Ch. Bouqueyran	Moulis
Ch. Brillette	Moulis
Ch. Capdeville	Listrac

Crus Bourgeois

Ch. Cap du Haut
Ch. Chasse-Spleen
Ch. Chevalier d'Arts
Ch. Citran-Clauzel
Co-operative (Grand Listra
Ch. Fonbadet
Ch. Fonréaud
Ch. Fourcas-Dupré
Ch. Fourcas-Hostein
Ch. Courant
Ch. Glana
Ch. Gloria
Ch. Grand-Poujeaux-Theil
Ch. L'Abbégorsse-de-Gorsse
Ch. Labégorce
Ch. Labégorce-Zédé
Ch. La Couronne
La Dame Blanche (the White Wine of Ch. du Taillan)
Ch. Lanessan
Ch. Larragay
Ch. Lartigue
Ch. de Lamarque
Ch. Malescasse
Ch. Marbuzet
Ch. Montbrun
Ch. Moulin-à-Vent
Ch. Paveil
Ch. de Pez
Ch. Phélan-Ségur
Ch. Siran
Ch. du Taillan
Ch. Villegeorge

Lama
Lama
Saint-E
Cantena
Moulis
Soussans-
Saint-Estèp
Saint-Estèph
Labarde
Le Taillan
Avensan

Ch. Fonplégade
Ch. Franc-Mayne
Ch. Grand-Mayne
Ch. Grand-Pontet
Ch. Guadet-St-Julien
Ch. la Carte
Ch. la Cluzière
Ch. la Dominique
Ch. La Marzelle
Ch. Larmande
Ch. Lasserre
Ch. La Tour Figeac
Ch. le Couvent
Ch. Mauvezin
Ch. Montesquieu
Ch. Pavie-Décesse
Ch. Pavillon-Cadet
Ch. Petit-Faurie-de-
 Soutard
Ch. Sansonnet
Ch. Soutard
Ch. Trimoulet
Ch. Troplong-Mondot
Ch. Yon Figeac
Ch. Clos la Madeleine

Ch. Les Grandes Muraillés
Ch. Jean-Faure
Ch. la Clotte
Ch. la Couspaude
Ch. Larcis-Ducasse
Ch. Lamarzelle-Figeac
Ch. Laroze
Ch. la Tour-du-Pin-Figeac
Ch. le Châtelet
Ch. le Prieuré
Ch. Moulin du Cadet
Ch. Pavie-Macquin
Ch. Petit-Faurie de
 Souchard
Ch. Ripeau
Ch. Saint-George-Côte-
 Pavie
Ch. Tetre-Daugay
Ch. Trois-Moulins
Ch. Villemaurine
Clos des Jacobins
Clos Saint-Martin
Clos Fleurus
Clos l'Eglise

POMEROL

Ch. Beauregard
Ch. Certan-Giraud
Ch. Certan-de-May
Ch. Gazin
Ch. La Conseillante
Ch. La Croix

Ch. Lafleur
Ch. Lafleur-Petrus
Ch. Lagrange
Ch. La Pointe
Ch. Latour-Pomerol
Clos de l'Eglise-Clinet

Ch. l'Evangile
Ch. Nénin
Ch. Petit-Village
Ch. Petrus

Ch. Rouget
Ch. Trotanoy
Vieux-Château-Certan

SAUTERNES

1855 Classification

Grand premièr cru	Communes
Ch. d'Yquem	Sauternes

Premiers crus

Ch. La Tour-Blanche	Bommes
Ch. Lafaurie-Peyraguey	Bommes
Ch. Rayne-Vigneau	Bommes
Ch. de Suduiraut	Preignac
Ch. Coutet	Barsac
Ch. Climens	Barsac
Ch. Rieussec	Fargues
Ch. Rabaud	Bommes
Ch. Guiraud	Sauternes

Deuxièmes Crus

Ch. de Myrat	Barsac
Ch. Doisy	Barsac
Ch. Doisy-Dubroca	Barsac
Ch. Doisy-Daëne	Barsac
Ch. Doisy-Védrines	Barsac
Ch. Peixotto	Bommes
Ch. d'Arche	Sauternes
Ch. Filhot	Sauternes

Deuxièmes Crus (*cont.*)	Communes
Ch. Broustet	Barsac
Ch. Nairac	Barsac
Ch. Caillou	Barsac
Ch. Suau	Barsac
Ch. de Malle	Preignac
Ch. Raymond-Lafon	Fargues
Ch. Lamothe	Sauternes

GRAVES

1959 *Classification*

Red Wines

Ch. Haut Brion	Pessac
Ch. Bouscaut	Cadaujac
Ch. Carbonnieux	Léognan
Domaine du Chevalier	Léognan
Ch. Fieuzal	Léognan
Ch. Haut-Bailly	Léognan
Ch. la Mission-Haut-Brion	Pessac
Ch. la Tour-Haut-Brion	Talence
Ch. la Tour-Martillac	Martillac
Ch. Malartic-Lagravière	Léognan
Ch. Olivier	Léognan
Ch. Pape Clément	Pessac
Ch. Smith-Haut-Lafitte	Martillac

White Wines

Ch. Bouscat	Cadaujac
Ch. la Tour Martillac	Martillac
Ch. Laville-Haut-Brion	Talence

White Wines (*cont.*)	**Communes**
Ch. Couhins	Villenave-d'Ornon
Ch. Carbonnieux	Léognan
Ch. Olivier	Léognan
Domaine de Chevalier	Léognan
Ch. Malartic-la-Gravière	Léognan

APPENDIX III

Vintage Chart

🦂

Alsace	1955; 1959; 1961; 1962; 1964; 1966; 1967; 1969
Bordeaux (White)	1928; 1929; 1934; 1937; 1945; 1947; 1949; 1952; 1953; 1955; 1959; 1961
(Red)	1928; 1934; 1945; 1947; 1949; 1950; 1952; 1953; 1955; 1959; 1961; 1962; 1964; 1966 ;
Burgundy (White)	1947; 1950; 1952; 1953; 1955; 1957; 1959; 1961; 1962; 1966; 1967; 1969
(Red)	1934; 1937; 1945; 1947; 1949; 1952; 1953; 1955; 1957; 1959; 1961; 1962; 1964; 1966; 1967; 1969
Côtes du Rhône	1945; 1947; 1949; 1950; 1952; 1955; 1957; 1961; 1964; 1966; 1967
Loire (Muscadet)	1964; 1966; 1967; 1969
(Anjou-Touraine)	1943; 1945; 1947; 1949; 1952; 1953; 1955; 1959; 1961; 1964; 1966; 1967; 1969
(Pouilly-Sancerre)	1961; 1962; 1964; 1966; 1967; 1969

Champagne	1949; 1952; 1955; 1959; 1961; 1962; 1964
Rhine	1952; 1953; 1955; 1957; 1958; 1959; 1964; 1966; 1967; 1969
Moselle	1953; 1958; 1959; 1964; 1966; 1967; 1969

I am not really in favour of vintage charts. I find that too many people tend to follow them slavishly to the last letter. No chart can ever be more than a guide, since every wine develops at a different rate. Clarets, for example, can take anything from ten to fifteen years to reach maturity, while German white wines are at their best within five to seven years of their vintage year.

It happens sometimes, too, that in an undistinguished year, an estate may produce an outstanding wine.

I remember dining a few years ago with Ronald Barton (the proprietor of Châteaux Langoa and Léoville-Barton at St Julien) when we discussed this question. To prove the point he gave me a 1944 to taste. Most of the wines of that year were averagely good, but this was a truly great and unforgettable bottle.

Therefore please use the above chart with prudence. In choosing a wine of any of the dates I have mentioned you will not go wrong. On the other hand, by adventuring in a so-called 'bad' year, you may, perhaps, unearth a treasure.

I cannot do better than to end by quoting the wise advice of a great French wine connoisseur, who said, 'As a general rule buy the minor growths of the great years, and the great growths of the lesser years.'

Index

Index